UNDER
BARNEGAT'S BEAM

UNDER

BARNEGAT'S BEAM

Light on Happenings Along the Jersey Shore

By BAYARD RANDOLPH KRAFT
1894-1956

O'DONNELL PUBLISHING

1979—Published with
permission of

MARION C. KRAFT

O'DONNELL PUBLISHING

THIRD PRINTING APRIL 1979
FOURTH PRINTING JULY 1979
FIFTH PRINTING MAY 1980

Copyright © 1960 Marion C. Kraft
PREPARED FOR PUBLICATION BY GEORGE H. ECKHARDT
DESIGNED BY LE ROY H. APPLETON
DISTRIBUTED BY APPLETON, PARSONS & CO., INC.
52 VANDERBILT AVENUE, NEW YORK 17, N. Y.
MANUFACTURED IN THE UNITED STATES OF AMERICA

This book is more than a collection of historical facts neatly arranged by an impartial observer. It is a labor of love, containing the sights, the sounds—even the flavors—of a way of life my father greatly admired and of a people he greatly loved. They, in return, were quick to bestow their affection on him, creating over the years an unshakeable bond of loyalty and trust. Fortunately, this mutual affection overflowed and my father found it impossible not to put it into words. What follows here is his tribute to his friends from—"T'other side of the Bay."

BAYARD R. KRAFT, JR.

FOREWORD

Mariners' charts show a strip of New Jersey coast, some twenty miles in length, as Long Beach. This is really an island separated from the mainland by a bay. The northern tip of this island has for a landmark one of the tallest and best known lighthouses in the world and the whole region was under the beam of this light.

This book concerns Long Beach, its history, traditions and people. And it embraces the adjacent mainland. It is a somewhat interesting account of discovery, settlement, Indians, Revolutionary War exploits, raiders, renegades, Tories, hardy lighthouse keepers, brave life savers, famous hotel proprietors: all mixed in with sundry shipwrecks and a bit of cooking.

Too often the traditions and legends of years are incorrect. Therefore early records have been diligently sought out and followed wherever possible. The photographs have been gathered over the years and most have never been used in a publication.

The author's good and honored friend, Mr. Nathaniel R. Ewan wrote, "Few of the many visitors who find the attractions of Long Beach to their liking are aware of the wealth of factual and traditional background that highlights the story of this elongated stretch of our Jersey coast line. Dominated by 'Old Barney,' its narrow outlines form a precarious barrier between the ocean and the less turbulent waters of Barnegat Bay. Its well advertised slogan, 'six miles at sea,' invests it with a marine atmosphere all its own and its many off-shore shoals aptly evoke the sinister title 'ocean graveyard.'

"One visions the flotsam and jetsam of shipwreck and the pathos of lost lives. No less are suggested well founded traditions of high seas pirates whose exploits can no more be ignored than persistent tales of smugglers and 'mooncussers,' who, with false lights, lured unsuspecting vessels ashore for what plunder they might afford. American Revolutionary privateers sailed within the tidal creeks and inlets and discharged their captured British cargoes onto an eagerly receptive mainland. Whaling was not the least of this area's activities. Certainly all this and more did much to enliven the lives of these virile baymen and seamen whose adventures have long awaited telling."

ACKNOWLEDGEMENTS

Friends made this volume possible; without their assistance and guidance, the accuracy and interest of these pages would have been impossible as most of the things mentioned or referred to are no longer in existence. Jerseymen all unless otherwise noted.

Norwood H. Andrews of Moorestown
F. Morse Archer Jr. of Moorestown
B. Newton Barber of Haddonfield
Captain Luther Carver, of Barnegat Light
Clarkson A. Cranmer, Esquire of Somerville
Mrs. Howard C. Darnell, of Moorestown
Burleigh B. Draper, of Haddonfield
Nathaniel R. Ewan, of Burlington
Francis Fenimore, of Hollywood, Florida
Jason L. Fenimore, of Wayne, Penna., now deceased
Captain Asher K. Fleming, of Barnegat Light
Clarence D. Gant, of Barnegat Light
Chris Halverson, of Barnegat Light
Alex H. Inman, of Manahawkin
Captain Jens T. Jensen, of Barnegat Light
Warren Jillson of Tuckerton
Mrs. Minnie D. Kelly, of Barnegat Light
Howard R. Kemble, of Camden
Mrs. Emmor H. Lee, of Moorestown, now deceased
Cyril Morand, of Longport
J. Howard Perrine, of Barnegat, now deceased
Winfield Predmore, of West Collingswood
Mrs. Henry Ridgely, of Dover, Delaware
Mrs. Joseph E. Roberts, of Haddonfield
Miss Marguerite Robinson, of Narberth, Penna.
Mrs. Gustav Rosser, of Philadelphia, Penna.
Eward Schoening, of Barnegat Light
Miss Hannah Severns, of Moorestown
Captain Ralph P. Smith, of Tuckerton

I am especially appreciative of their many kindnesses

BAYARD R. KRAFT
Moorestown, New Jersey

CONTENTS

	Foreword	vii
	Acknowledgments	viii
Chapter I	THE GATEWAY TO LONG BEACH	1

Clamtown becomes Tuckerton. The Clamtown Sailcar. A Quaker Meeting House and a Wireless Station. Decoys and Boats. The Third Port of Entry. Tuckerton Schooners and Ebenezer Tucker. Edward Andrews and Willow Landing.

Chapter II	"LONG LAND WATER" OF THE INDIANS BECOMES THE NEW JERSEY OF THE BRITISH	9

"Nova Caesarea" — New Jersey. The Keith and Lawrence Lines.

Chapter III	THE INDIANS	13

The First Indian Reservation in the United States. The Last Indian in the Area: Lashy — and His Daughter Indian Ann. Dark Spots in the Fields Yield Skeletons of Tall Indians.

Chapter IV	OLD "BARNIGATE" BEACH	21

The Ancient Cedars of New Jersey. Whales and Whalers of Long Beach. The Pirate of the New Jersey Coast: Richard Worley.

Chapter V	THE GALLANT WORK OF THE VOLUNTEER LIFE BOAT CREWS	27
Chapter VI	BARNEGAT LIFE BOAT STATION	31
Chapter VII	LIFE BOAT STATIONS ON LONG BEACH	37
Chapter VIII	"OLD BARNEY"—BARNEGAT LIGHTHOUSE	41

The First Barnegat Light. General George Gordon Meade and the Barnegat Light. The Keepers.

Chapter IX	THE EARLY BOARDING HOUSES ON LONG BEACH ISLAND	61
	The "Philadelphia Company House." "Mansion of Health." The "Ashley House." The "Long Beach House."	
Chapter X	BARNEGAT CITY AND ITS HOTELS	68
	The "Oceanic Hotel." The "Sunset Hotel." "The Social." "Barnegat City Inn."	
Chapter XI	BEACH HAVEN IN THE 1880's	72
	"Club House." The "Parry House." The "Engleside."	
Chapter XII	HARVEY CEDARS	75
	The Schooner Yacht "Sans Souci"	
Chapter XIII	BUILDER OF BARNEGAT SNEAK BOXES— J. H. PERRINE	78
Chapter XIV	THE SECOND PROPRIETOR OF THE OLD HARVEY CEDARS HOTEL	81
	Mementoes of the Sea.	
Chapter XV	THE END OF THE FIRST HARVEY CEDARS HOTEL	84
	Floral Sneak Boxes.	
Chapter XVI	A FAMILY DEDICATED TO A HOTEL	87
	A Distinguished Guest.	
Chapter XVII	HARVEY CEDARS LANDMARKS OF THE PAST	89
	The "Seven Cedars Club." The "Peahala Club."	
Chapter XVIII	HARVEY CEDARS FIFTY YEARS AGO	92
Chapter XIX	RAILROADS AND ROADS TO LONG BEACH	95
Chapter XX	A FASCINATING ENDEAVOR—TRACING OLD NAMES	99
	Forks of Little Egg Harbour. John Bacon — Outlaw. Batsto and Bog Iron.	
Chapter XXI	BARNEGAT COOKERY	108
	Authorities Consulted	117
	Index	118

ILLUSTRATIONS

Bayard Randolph Kraft at Long Beach	53
Barnegat Lighthouse and Keepers' Dwelling in September, 1919	53
Barnegat Pier railroad station in 1915	54
Former home of "Indian Ann" Roberts at Dingletown, N. J.	54
Captain Bond's famous "Long Beach House," below Beach Haven, in 1908	55
The "new" house of the PEAHALA CLUB, on beach at Peahala, in 1903	55
The enlarged Harvey Cedars Hotel in 1923	56
Batsto bog iron fire-back in Ridgely homestead, Dover, Delaware	56
Famed figurehead west of Harvey Cedars Hotel porch in 1902	57
Italian Barque "FORTUNA" which came ashore January 18, 1910	57
The "Tar Pot," Engine No. 2, of the Manahawkin and Long Beach Transportation Company, in 1906	58
The "Dummy" built for summer season of 1893	58
ASHLEY HOUSE, Barnegat City, in 1887	59
Snow and the old Harvey Cedars Hotel on March 21, 1892	59
Captain Samuel Forman Perrine, Jr. at the wheel of the schooner-yacht "Sans Souci" in the early 1890's	60
Barnegat Lightship	60

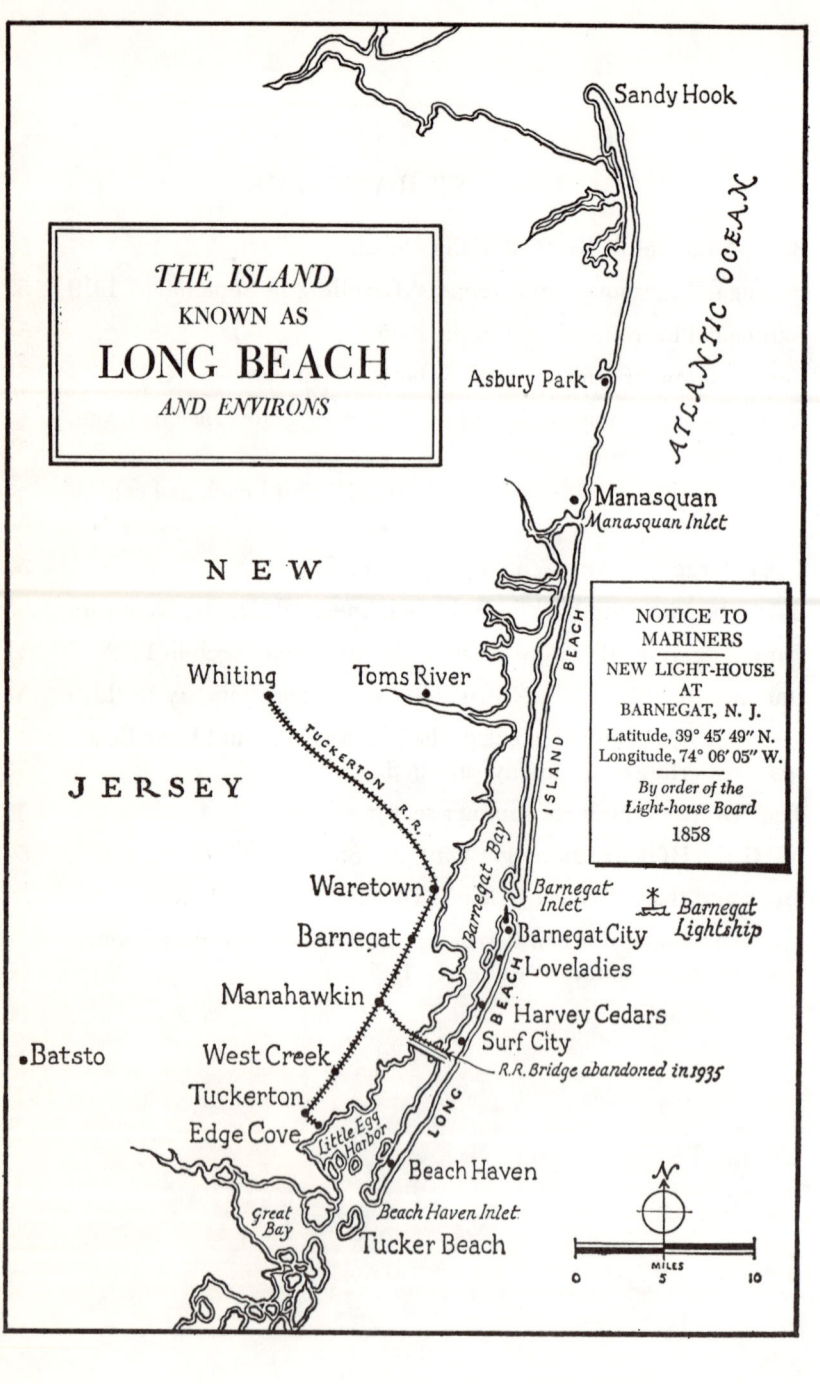

CHAPTER I

THE GATEWAY TO LONG BEACH

We begin our story with a New Jersey town of many names. Were you to consult Scott's Atlas, published in 1799, you would find it designated "Clamtown." On a modern map it would be Tuckerton. These are only two of the numerous names by which it has been known through more than two and one-half centuries and each name is interwoven in its history.

Thomas F. Gordon, in his "History of New Jersey," published in 1834, refers to Tuckerton in this manner: "post town and port of entry for Little Egg Harbour district, about 35 miles S.E. of Mount Holly, 65 from Trenton, and 189 N.E. from W.C. (Washington, D.C.), situate on a narrow tongue of land, projecting into the marsh of Little Egg Harbour Bay, Little Egg Harbour t(own)-ship, Burlington Co., contains between 30 and 40 dwellings, 4 taverns, 5 stores, 2 Methodist churches, a Quaker meeting house. It lies upon a navigable stream, called Shord's Mill Branch, 6 miles from the Bay, whence wood scows and flats ascend to the town. There is a large business done here in timber and cord-wood; and salt is, or was manufactured in the vicinity. The town is frequented during the summer by many persons for the benefit of sea-bathing, &c. A stage plies regularly between it and Philadelphia."

Tuckerton was more than a hundred and twenty-five years old when Gordon described it since it had been settled by the Friends in the 1690's and a Quaker Meeting had been established by 1702. The locality took its name from this meeting house—"Little Egg Harbour." Later it was known as "Middle of the Shore," both of these being regional rather than place names. The town itself was referred to as "Quakertown." A few old maps show the village as "Fishtown."

The present name, Tuckerton, was decided upon at a township feast in 1798. Ebenezer Tucker, a remarkable man, invited the entire community to a great dinner of boiled beef and pork, boiled turnips and potatoes, beans and rye bread. The dinner was given by this entrepreneur for the express purpose of having the thriving town named for himself.

Clamtown Becomes Tuckerton

After 1800 the name appears on maps as Tuckertown, Tuckinton and Tuckerton, evidently depending upon the whim of the map maker. The enterprise and ingenuity of Ebenezer Tucker seemed to inspire the town people and long survived him.

An increasing number of persons frequented the town during the summer season for the benefit of sea-bathing. Long Beach, the island across the Bay, attracted more and more summer visitors. The stage spoken of by Gordon gave way to the railroad. Many of these visitors came to Tuckerton by rail and were ferried across the Bay in boats. Tuckerton became the gateway to Long Beach.

This traffic steadily increased. In 1872 the railroad built a short spur from its mainline at Tuckerton to a spot on the mainland bay shore called Edge Cove. This was before the railroad bridge was built across Manahawkin Bay connecting Long Beach with the mainland.

Railroad transportation for passengers, baggage and freight bound for Long Beach then ended at Edge Cove. The steamboats "Barclay" and "Pohatcong" carried passengers and freight across to Beach Haven. After arrival at Beach Haven passengers for boarding houses at other locations on the island were sailed up the Bay to their destinations. All in all, it made the trip a full day's journey.

When direct rail service to Long Beach was established in June, 1886, the year in which the railroad bridge across the Bay was completed, the Edge Cove spur was abandoned. However, only the switch connecting the spur to the mainline was removed. The rails remained across the meadow as did one flat car.

The Clamtown Sailcar

Baymen — oystermen and clammers — continued to use the Edge Cove dock. Here they cleaned, sorted, counted and packed their oysters, clams and fish. They had been quick to grasp the opportunity afforded by the railroad in making it possible for them to ship their seafood to profitable city markets. They were no longer dependent on coastal schooners. But when the spur to Edge Cove was abandoned they were confronted by the problem of how to convey their sacks, boxes and barrels each day from the dock to the mainline of the railroad.

The problem was solved in true bayman fashion. The old flat car was converted into a land-going ship! It was fully rigged with a mast and sails. The old spur line tracks offered a smooth and reefless channel. So expert were these baymen in sailing this flat car that few trips were missed no matter from which direction the winds blew. The sight of a flat car — under full sail — and loaded with boxes and barrels — speeding across the meadow baffled visitors.

The Clamtown sailcar, as it was called, was unique and served the baymen for several years. Had there not been an accident it would probably have run indefinitely. In those days Tuckerton made much of celebrating Halloween. On such a night some of the older boys decided upon a ride on the sailcar. They were probably too eager for speed and the sailcar jumped the track at a curve and went into a ditch. There some of its rusting parts may still be seen.

A Quaker Meeting House and a Wireless Station

"Meeting House Pond" is two miles south of Tuckerton on the Wireless Road. This pond was first to freeze in winter and was used by children for skating. It was so named because there was once a meeting house in the nearby woods. The pond is part of Caldwell's Run.

It may seem incongruous to speak of an ancient Quaker meeting house and Wireless Road in the same sentence but Tuckerton did have the highest wireless tower in the world. It was the second highest man-made structure of its time, only surpassed by the Eiffel Tower in Paris.

The Tuckerton Wireless Tower, known throughout the world, was on Hickory Island. Construction was started in 1912 and completed in 1914. It was built by a German company and at the time was the highest landmark along the Atlantic coast. The huge triangular open tower originally extended eight hundred and fifty feet above the meadow. Some years later, while the tower was still in use, seventy-five feet were removed from its top to increase its power. It was a wonderful beacon and landmark with its flashing red blinker light. In clear weather, either by day or night, the structure and installation could be seen for miles.

The Wireless Tower at Tuckerton is gone. On December 28, 1955, wreckers cut several supporting cables and the structure crashed to the earth. There seem to be plans to develop the hundreds of acres surrounding the tower site into a resort. If this is done some of the houses will be no larger than the huge concrete anchors that held the supporting cables of the tower.

Speaking of anchors recalls Anchor, or Anchoring, Island often mentioned in the log books of coasting vessels and shown on old maps. The Island, some fifteen acres in area, was located in the Bay opposite Great Egg Harbor Inlet, an inlet which has been closed for years and now has new channels on either side of the old location.

Anchoring Island was washed away many years ago and some twenty feet of salt water today rush across the old site. The Island's name was very appropriate since vessels anchored in its lee to wait out a blow or for a change in tides. It was a natural haven for sailing ships in bad weather.

Decoys and Boats

The Tuckerton area was justly famous as a center of the art of making decoys for hunting. Skilled artisans made decoys of wood, tin or iron to represent snipe, ducks or geese. Harry Shourds had a national reputation for making various types of decoys and shipped them all over North America. John Bartlett and Ernest Smith were also outstanding decoy makers. Specimens of their skill are now collectors' items.

What are now called motor boats were known as launches prior to World War I. Like the early automobiles, the engines coughed, smoked, balked and sometimes failed completely. Jason Fenimore, of Harvey Cedars and Manahawkin, had a most appropriate name for his launch — "No Go" — which was boldly painted on the bow. It was an event when it returned to its dock under its own power and a pushing pole was part of the regular equipment.

Sailboats were very important in the pre-motorboat era, and sailing them called for great skill. Captain Samuel J. Smith, of Tuckerton, ferried all of the lumber needed for the construction of the Baldwin Hotel Annex across the Bay in his cat yacht "Broadbill." Captain Will Smith carried the mail across the Bay from Tuckerton to the south end of Long Beach. He usually sailed the mail across in his boat. But in winter, when the Bay was frozen over, he pushed his way across in a sneak box fitted with brass runners. One winter, when the Bay ice was eighteen inches thick for several weeks, he walked the several miles back and forth with the mail.

The Third Port of Entry

Tuckerton has the distinction of having been the third Port of Entry in the United States. After the formation of this Nation, Philadelphia, the then largest city, became the first Port of Entry. This was followed by New York and then by Tuckerton. The commission is dated March 21, 1791, and is signed by George Washington as President and Thomas Jefferson as Secretary of State.

Ebenezer Tucker was the first Collector of the Port of Tuckerton and since his time the Collector's Office has always been in the home of the man holding the appointment. Collectors following Tucker were Charles Bartlett, John T. Burtan, Samuel Bartlett, George W. Mathis, George Crammer, James E. Otis and William Allen, Jr. Several of these men held office when more than a hundred schooners registered Tuckerton as their home port.

Tuckerton Schooners and Ebenezer Tucker

Great forests of fine hardwood trees which once surrounded Tuckerton made it an important ship building center, thriving under the enterprise of early Quaker settlers. Tuckerton built schooners were well thought of by salt water sailors and many were engaged in a substantial coastal trade.

Bartlett's Coaling Dock was located on the west bank of Tuckerton Creek about midway to the Bay, and a century ago was a place of considerable importance. Here teams brought their loads of cord wood and large wagons brought their bushels of charcoal. Two masted schooners carried this fuel to Philadelphia and Boston to heat homes. All that now remains of this once busy dock are a few rotting timbers and short piling stumps in the water.

According to the records of the Post Office Department a post office was established at Tuckerton on August 18, 1797. The early postmasters and their dates of appointment were: Reuben Tucker, August 18, 1797; William Watson, February 25, 1801; David Stoute, July 1, 1805; and Ebenezer Tucker, December 28, 1805. He served until May 8, 1840.

Ebenezer Tucker performed many services for his community, state and nation. He served in the Continental Army during the Revolution and was elected to Congress in 1825-1829, serving in the Nineteenth and Twentieth Congresses. He was appointed a Judge of the Common Pleas Court and Orphan's Court and was a Justice of the Court of Quarter Sessions.

Around 1800 he built and established "Union Inn" at Tuckerton, a portion of which is incorporated in the present "Carlton House." He owned several schooners, some of which were engaged in the West Indies trade, loading lumber at Tuckerton and returning with sugar and molasses. In addition to this he was one of the original directors of "The Burlington County Bank," organized in 1837 at Medford, Burlington County.

Ebenezer Tucker died September 5, 1845, and is buried in the Methodist Cemetery at Tuckerton, his grave being marked by the dominating obelisk of the burying ground.

Edward Andrews and Willow Landing

The buildings at Main and Water Streets, Tuckerton, are supported by portions of the foundations of the original Edward Andrews grist mill. Tuckerton is like that—the new is built upon the old and looks to the old for support and finds it.

Edward Andrews, the reputed founder of what is now Tuckerton, was born on the 16th of the First Month, 1677. When he grew up he acquired some five hundred acres on the east side of Tuckerton Lake. He married Sarah Ong, a daughter of Sarah Ong, Sr., believed to have been a widow at the time of her daughter's marriage. The wedding took place at the home of Thomas Revell in Burlington on February 8, 1694.

Edward Andrews tired of taking his grain to Burlington to have it ground and in about 1704 erected a grist mill at the beaver dam, where today's shore road curves around the south end of Tuckerton Lake. This was the first grist mill in the area.

In 1708 Edward Andrews conveyed two acres of land on the east side of the Lake, well back from the road, to the Trustees of the local Quaker Meeting. A one story meeting house was immediately built on this land, John Crammer being the head carpenter. This original meeting house remained in constant use until 1865 when it was torn down and the present meeting house erected. Meetings are still held here at 11 a.m. on First Days during the summer months.

The window frames of the first meeting house were brought from England, the small diamond shaped panes of glass being set in lead. These leaden window frames were taken down and hidden during the Revolution so that they would not be seized and melted down for shot.

Tuckerton, like most mainland towns near salt water, had its salt works during the Revolution. These were located on the Bay Shore so that a wind-mill could pump salt water into the boiler and ultimately into the salt pans. British restrictions and taxes had made the importation of salt prohibitive, so the Colonists manufactured their own salt by the simple process of evaporating sea water. Many New Jersey bog iron furnaces cast large shallow salt pans for the final evaporation. Old maps of Tuckerton show the road leading to the salt works as Salt Works Lane. It has now been renamed Marine Street. The largest salt works at Tuckerton were operated by a substantial company and produced some eight hundred pounds of salt a year.

Boats still tie up at Willow Landing, the grand old name for the town dock about a block down Tuckerton Creek from where Andrews' Mill once stood. Tuckerton Creek was known to the Indians as "Pohatcong" after the lake on the upper side of the beaver dam. Later it had many names, being generally known by the name of the then mill owner. On various maps it is shown as Andrews' Mill Creek, Jacob Andrews' Mill Creek, Shourd's Mill Creek, Shord's Mill Branch and plain Mill Creek.

The huge willow trees that once shaded Willow Landing, and gave the place its name, are all gone — the last twisted trunk blew down in June of 1950. The Landing once extended for some distance along the creek bank. It was a scene of great activity with business being done in large timber, lumber, cord-wood, split shingles, charcoal, salt, flax and molasses.

Boarding Captain Smith's boat at Willow Landing and going down Tuckerton Creek to the Bay was an interesting and rewarding experience. As we came out of the Creek, to the left, beyond some cottages, we saw Gaunnt's Point, named for Hananiah Gaunnt, husband of Ann Ridgway Gaunnt, Tuckerton's distinguished female Quaker preacher.

Down the channel a couple of miles, on the left, was a large island, once easily recognized by a big brick chimney of the abandoned mossbunker fertilizer plant on Storey's Island. This landmark crashed to the ground early in April, 1954.

Across the channel from the fertilizer plant site was a broad salt meadow. This meadow has been called Fox Burrow since before the Revolution. Many years ago the drifting ice fields piled the meadow sod up at this point in such a manner that it was above high water and even above storm tides. Foxes made their dens or burrows in this higher meadow land. The place is sometimes referred to as Foxborough.

Not very far from Fox Burrow is another location where a Revolutionary War name still applies to a winding back channel. This is "Soldier's Hole" and it may be found on present day charts. The Continental Army established a sentry post on the back of this narrow channel to observe ships entering Little Egg Harbor Inlet. The location was ideal for this purpose since the view was unobstructed. The observation point was comparatively safe because it was impossible to reach Soldier's Hole except in a small boat and then only by one familiar with the shoals of the winding channel.

CHAPTER II

"LONG LAND WATER" OF THE INDIANS BECOMES
THE NEW JERSEY OF THE BRITISH

We shall probably never know the name of the first European to sight the New Jersey shore line and Long Beach. Most historians today credit Henry Hudson with the distinction of having been the first to land.

As will be remembered, he was an Englishman employed by the Dutch East Indies Company. On April 4, 1609, he sailed in search of a Northwest Passage to India. His single ship, the "Half Moon," was a two-masted vessel of about eighty tons, manned by a crew of twenty.

Hudson sighted Newfoundland, then coasted down the shore, landing near the present Portland, Maine. He then rounded Cape Cod and sailed southward as far as the Virginia Capes. There he turned about and entered the Delaware Bay on August 28, 1609. Unable to locate deep water to his liking, and fearing the shoals, he again put to sea and sailed up the New Jersey coast.

It is said that he anchored off Barnegat Inlet for the night of September 2, 1609. The next day he dropped anchor at Sandy Hook in four and one-half fathoms of water and twelve hundred feet from the beach.

A landing was made on Friday, September 4, 1609. Accounts of this event differ. Some claim that Hudson first sent a small boat manned by a few of his crew to ascertain whether the Indians were friendly. Others contend that Hudson led the landing party and was the first European to step ashore on the soil of New Jersey.

Hudson remained at Sandy Hook for eight days during which the first hostile act on the part of the Indians occurred. On Sunday, September 6, 1609, one of the sailors, John Coleman or Colman, a member of a small boat crew, was shot through the neck by an arrow and died. Two other members of the boat party were wounded.

Again accounts differ. Some contend that the small boat was close to shore and that the attacking Indians were hidden in the foliage. Others hold that Hudson was in charge and that his boat was pursued by several canoes carrying a war party of Indians.

In any event John Coleman was killed and buried at the foot of one of the many gnarled cedar trees that lined the shores of Sandy Hook for so many years. This was most probably the first encounter between Europeans and American Indians within the limits of the present State of New Jersey.

But many Europeans must have sighted the New Jersey coast line and Long Beach before Henry Hudson. And it is even possible that some of these mariners were shipwrecked on the treacherous shoals.

John Cabot, a Venetian, with his son Sebastian, sailed from Bristol, England, in 1497, in the service of Henry VII. From Newfoundland the Cabots sailed down the eastern coast of North America as far as Cape Hatteras and possibly as far as Florida. This fact seems to have been ignored by most historians. The Cabots must have sailed along and sighted the New Jersey Coast and Long Beach.

A Florentine, Giovanni Verranzo, commanding a squadron of three vessels for King Francis I of France, sailed along the Atlantic coast of North America. It is known that he sailed into New York Bay in 1523. In the same year a Portuguese, Estevan Gomez, sailing for Emperor Charles V of Portugal, is believed to have done some exploring along the shores of both the Delaware and Hudson Rivers.

It is not only possible but quite probable that the intrepid Norse navigators sailed along this coast as early as 1000 A.D. These men may have landed on the New Jersey shores. Some day we will probably know whether these seamen were the first to discover New Jersey, some hundreds of years before the present accepted dates.

"Nova Caesarea" — New Jersey

What is now the State of New Jersey had many names in the past. The Indians called it "Skaabee" or "Scheyichbi," generally translated as "Long Land Water." The Swedes knew it as "Nye Svierge" or "New Sweden," along with their settlements on the west banks of the Delaware. The Dutch called it "Nova Belgia," and when included with New York it became "New Netherlands."

The flags of three monarchic governments flew over what is now New Jersey. That of the Swedes until 1654, when the Dutch took control for ten years. The British then conquered the Dutch and held sway for more than a century.

The British, under Colonel Richard Nicolls, seized "New Netherlands" from the Dutch on August 27, 1664 (O. S.) in the name of the Duke of York. Colonel Nicolls called the land west of the Hudson River, including New Jersey, "Albania."

On June 23 and 24, 1664 (O. S.), James, Duke of York, had granted the land between the Hudson and Delaware Rivers to two royal favorites: John, Lord Berkeley, privy councillor and Baron of Stratton: and Sir George Carteret, who had been treasurer of the Royal Navy.

The land was to be known as "Nova Caesarea" or "New Jersey," as a compliment to Carteret who had successfully defended the Isle of Jersey in the Puritan Civil War of 1643.

After the land division was agreed upon, Carteret became Proprietor of East New Jersey and Lord Berkeley became Proprietor of West New Jersey.

Colonel Nicolls, while administering the affairs of New York, had granted licenses to several settlers from the New Haven Colony, in Connecticut, to purchase large tracts of land in northern New Jersey from the Indians.

The settlers from New England came down, took up their lands and proceeded to make their own laws to govern themselves. Finally, in a letter dated November 25, 1672, the Duke of York annulled these grants in order to solidify the Colony. However, many North New Jersey settlers who held their lands under grants from Colonel Nicolls refused to pay quit-rents to the Proprietors.

After many conflicts with the settlers, the Proprietors, in 1702, surrendered the governing powers back to the Crown and New Jersey became a Royal Colony under the administration of Lord Cornbury, Royal Governor of New York.

The Colony of New Jersey continued to be governed by the Royal Governor of New York until 1738, when, in order to appease a rising resentment, particularly among the farmers, New Jersey was given its own governor.

Lord Berkeley disposed of his portion of New Jersey in 1675. After much discussion, George Keith, Surveyor-General of East Jersey, in 1687, was ordered by the Proprietors to run a dividing line between East and West New Jersey.

The Keith and Lawrence Lines

The Keith Line was corrected by John Chapman in 1721. Then the line dividing East and West New Jersey was definitely established, and in part re-located, by a survey made by John Lawrence in 1745.

Both the Keith and Lawrence Lines are shown on all old maps of New Jersey and are quite often found on present day maps since the Lines were used as the boundaries of many large land grants and conveyances.

The base point of both these Lines was at the end of Long Beach. It was marked by a stone but this monument was washed away by the sea many years ago and its original location is now well out in deep water.

The Keith Line was run from the east side of Little Egg Harbour, north by West. The beginning point was 41° 40′, North Latitude. It was run about sixty miles in accordance with a deed dated July 1, 1676.

Both Lines begin at the same point on the sea coast, with the Lawrence Line bearing slightly to the north. The starting point was arrived at by agreement and was described as follows, "the south partition point being the most southardly point on the east side of Little Egg Harbour in a map of said tract of land."

New Jersey's northern boundary line, between it and New York, was in dispute from the very beginning of colonization and was not finally settled until 1769 when a commission survey was accepted by both Colonies.

CHAPTER III

THE INDIANS

An estimated seven to ten thousand Indians lived in the present New Jersey when the first white settlers arrived. These Indians were of the Lenni Lenape tribe, an Indian name which has been variously translated as meaning "Our Men," "Important Men" and "Original People." Later they were known as the Delawares.

The Delawares, generally speaking, were noncombatant savages, being considered among other Indian tribes as "Wise Men" and "Peacemakers." Friendly relations with these Delawares enabled the colonists to enjoy peaceful possession of their lands. The manner in which the Indians were treated by the early settlers in New Jersey is to the everlasting credit of the Colonists.

Despite the fact that these settlers arrived with royal grants and deeds for their lands, they negotiated with the chiefs of the tribes then occupying the territory. The settlers paid the Indians agreed purchase prices and the Indians in turn executed consideration deeds signed by their chiefs. Many of these deeds are a matter of record and are highly prized by their present owners.

Each spring the Delawares of New Jersey made their annual migration to the seashore where they fared bountifully on the flesh of birds, birds' eggs, fish and shell fish, which were so abundant in that area.

Several well established Indian paths or trails crossed the Province to the seacoast, and these, together with water courses, were used by the Indians. The best known New Jersey trails were the Minisink, which went in a southeasterly direction to within a short distance of the present Elizabeth; the Peapack, which crossed the northern part of the Province from east to west; and the Burlington and Shamong paths, the latter going down to Cape May.

The shell piles at certain locations on the mainland of New Jersey reveal the great quantities of oysters, clams and mussels that were dried, smoked and taken inland by the Indians for winter use. Discs for making wampum were also cut out of the clam and mussel shells.

The New Jersey Indians knew nothing about evaporating sea-water to obtain salt. Dried clams were used for both flavoring and meat. That the settlers learned to use dried clams in the same manner is evidenced by the fact that during the Revolution British prisoners of war protested against dozens of dried clams a day in lieu of meat.

There are Indian shell piles at Tuckerton and Brigantine. The piles vary in height or thickness from a couple of feet to more than ten; in length from twenty feet to several hundred and in width from five feet to more than twenty. During the years farmers have carted hundreds of wagon loads of these oyster, clam and mussel shells from these old Indian piles and have scattered them over their fields and plowed them under in order to lime their soil. It is claimed that when Indians planted corn along the coast a handful of shells or a clump of mussels was placed beneath each hill of corn.

New World plants such as potatoes, tomatoes, corn, peanuts and tobacco were planted by the Indians in regularly cultivated plots. They were also fond of the abundant wild cranberries, blackberries, whortleberries and strawberries. Most of the Indian cooking was done in clay pots with pieces of bark or cedar wood serving as dishes.

A small species of pointed ear dog appears to have been the only domesticated animal known to the New Jersey Indians. This dog was used for protection, hunting and even for food. It had an honored place in many ceremonies.

The Lenni Lenape were a fine Indian tribe, friendly and quite easy for the white man to live beside. But this very friendliness was their undoing since between the white man's diseases, to which they quickly succumbed, and their craving for intoxicating liquor, the Indians of New Jersey went down hill fast.

These Indians originally knew nothing about intoxicating liquor and the Dutch and Swedes are credited with introducing it to them. The Proprietors of New Jersey, as well as many early settlers, did their best to protect the Indians. At a very early date the Assembly of the Province passed legislation forbidding the sale, barter or giving strong drink to the Indians.

The First Indian Reservation in the United States

Concern for the plight of the Indians of New Jersey brought about the early establishment of the first Indian Reservation in America. An

Act creating this Reservation was passed by the Legislature of the Province of New Jersey on August 12, 1758.

In pursuance of this Act, the commissioners obtained releases and grants from the Indians, of their rights and claims to all lands in the Province. The commissioners also purchased a tract of land, called Edge Hillock, in the township of Evesham, County of Burlington, "containing three thousand and forty-four acres, on which the Indian town, known by the name of 'Brotherton', is erected." The deed, made to Governor Bernard and the commissioners, bears the date 29th of August, 1758.

This deed was made out to Governor Francis Bernard and Commissioners Andrew Johnson, Richard Salter, Charles Read, John Stevens, William Foster, and Jacob Spicer; who purchased the tract from Benjamin Spicer for seven hundred and forty pounds, Proclamation money. The boundary lines of the Reservation were marked with stone monuments some of which are still in position. Governor Bernard named the Reservation "Brotherton."

By this time there were very few Indians left in New Jersey south of the Raritan River so that there were never more than a few hundred living on the Reservation. Mr. Nathaniel R. Ewan informed me that he had seen the old account books of Atsion Furnace and that these showed that some Indians from the Brotherton Reservation worked there since the entries were for goods purchased at the company store and to be paid for out of the worker's salary. It is believed that Indians from the Reservation also worked at nearby Taunton Furnace. Atsion itself is an old Indian name, the village and furnace being named for the Assiyunk, or Atsionks, a small tribe living in that vicinity. Atsion Furnace was built about 1766, as were Batsto, Taunton and Etna Furnaces.

By 1801 the number of Indians dwelling on the Reservation had dwindled to some sixty-five adults. These Indians were invited by their kin at New Stockbridge, near Lake Oneida, New York State, to join them there. The invitation was accepted and the New Jersey Indians petitioned the Legislature to sell the Reservation and turn the money over to them. The necessary legislation was quickly passed and commissioners were appointed to divide the Reservation into tracts of about one hundred acres each.

Several suits and claims were filed by the heirs of the original owners claiming that title to the land reverted to them when it was abandoned as an Indian Reservation. But, after proper advertising, and in accordance with the legislation, a public auction was held at the tavern at Pipers Corner, on May 25, 1802. The various tracts were sold to the highest bidders with prices ranging from one and one-half to five dollars an acre.

The Indians made an additional claim for "Hunting and Fishing Rights" which they contended did not run with the land and had never been sold. And many purchasers of tracts claimed that the Indian Reservation Land was free of all taxes. It took several years and considerable litigation to straighten out all claims.

In the end the Indians received the funds from the sale of the land as well as a sum paid by the State for the hunting and fishing rights. The courts decreed that parcels of land sold from the Indian Reservation were taxable. Thus the first Indian Reservation in the United States ended in a manner equitable to all.

The Indians at New Stockbridge were not contented there and in 1832 moved westward to the Fox River area in Wisconsin, some going to Statesburgh and some to Green Bay. In the early 1800's several Indians continued to make their annual spring visits to the Tuckerton area to fish and gather oysters and clams.

Today's Indian Mills is the "Brotherton" named in the Act of Legislature setting up the first Indian Reservation. The burial grounds of the Reservation Indians adjoins the old Indian Mills school house, a mile or so from the present village of that name.

The Last Indian in the Area
Lashy — and His Daughter Indian Ann

The last Indian brave in the Tuckerton area was "Lashy," whose full name was Elisha Ashatama or Lasha Tamar. I obtained this information from Captain Ralph Parker Smith who was born in Tuckerton and familiar with its lore and history. Mr. L. T. Blackman, also of Tuckerton, informed me that his grand-father, as a boy, had talked with this Indian.

Like so many Indians, Lashy's fondness for the white man's fire water caused his death. On a night in 1833, while "under the influence," Lashy fell into the mill pond at Tuckerton and was drowned. He is buried in the Tuckerton Methodist Cemetery.

The stories of Lashy and his family are so enmeshed in the traditions of the Tuckerton-Burlington County area that it is extremely difficult to separate legend from fact. It is said that his mother was Nancy Ashatama, whose daughter, of the same name, migrated and settled in New Stockbridge, New York, in 1801. Lashy is believed to have been chief of the Brotherton Reservation Indians and to have led the migration to New Stockbridge. The persistent story is that he was dissatisfied with the New York Reservation and walked back to Burlington County. Others contend that he never left Burlington County.

At one time he did occupy a log cabin on the John Woolman farm near Rancocas. It is believed that he went to the shore in the neighborhood of Tuckerton after this. During his stay at the Woolman farm, or during one of his visits there, his daughter, later known as Indian Ann, was born in 1805. The identity of Indian Ann's mother, who was a full blooded Indian, is unknown. Some say she was Patty, Lashy's wife.

In 1812 Lashy disappeared and was gone for five years. Upon his return he claimed that he had been one of the crew of the "Chesapeake." On June 1, 1813, the U. S. Frigate "Chesapeake," 38 guns, with a green crew commanded by Captain James Lawrence, engaged the British Frigate "Shannon," 58 guns. This was a disastrous engagement, all of the "Chesapeake's" officers were killed and the ship captured. If Lashy really was a member of the "Chesapeake" crew his absence could be explained. In any event his wife, Patty, thinking herself a widow, had married a mulatto, whom Lashy drove away on his return.

The date of Indian Ann's birth is fixed in the affidavit of her son, John Roberts, Jr., whose enlistment papers in the Union Army during the Civil War are a matter of record. He was a member of "A" Company, 22nd Regiment of Colored Troops, and died of service connected injuries or disease in 1864 in the Army Hospital, Yorktown, Virginia. As a result of his services, Indian Ann received a pension from 1870 to the time of her death, in her 90th year, in December of 1894.

She is believed to have been married twice, her first husband having been Peter Green, a freed slave. Her second husband was John Roberts, a Negro, who was one of the founders of the A.M.E. Church at Dingletown, on the Tabernacle-Chatsworth Road. This church building was torn down some twenty-five years ago but the overgrown cemetery with a few neglected tombstones identify the site of this once well attended church.

Through the efforts of Mr. Nathaniel R. Ewan, the papers of the grave digger at the Methodist cemetery at Tabernacle were located and on the rough sketch of burial lots and graves there was found one designated "Indian Ann." The grave was readily located and the Burlington County Historical Society, in 1945, placed a modest marker on the grave of the County's last native American.

Indian Ann had other children in addition to the Civil War soldier, some say as many as seven, but nothing is known of them. Both Lashy and his daughter, Indian Ann, were skilled basket weavers and earned a small income selling them.

Two things are certain, according to the few people who can still recall Indian Ann. She had the classical features and copper colored skin of the true Indian and inherited her father's great fondness for the white man's firewater. Her well built house in the settlement of Dingletown, near Indian Mills, still stands. This was built by her with accrued pension money in around 1883.

Indian Ann at one time had two white dogs alike as two peas in a pod. She was annoyed by people constantly asking their names and how she told them apart. Her reply was always the same, "I know and they know — that's enough for anyone to know." What she did not tell people was that one dog was actually named "I Know" and the other was named "They Know."

Dark Spots in the Fields Yield Skeletons of Tall Indians

In 1949, Mr. Warren A. Jillson related the following account of discovering an Indian burying ground to me:

"In the early 1870's, my grandfather, Samuel Jillson, with his twin sons Alfred and Arthur, moved down from Lynn, Massachusetts, and purchased the present Jillson farm. Arthur Jillson was my father. The brothers had been taxidermists and naturalists in Massachusetts.

"The move to the New Jersey seashore area was made to enable the sons to regain their health by farming and outdoor life. The young men found the adjacent farms more interesting than the one they occupied and roamed them at will.

"One of these adjacent farms was the Ridgway place, then occupied by Miss Annie Ridgway and her bachelor brothers, Alfred and Job. The Jillson brothers spent most of their Sundays on the Ridgway farm, going over the fields again and again, seeking and finding Indian relics for their extensive collections.

"The other farm was known as the Courtney Farm of Revolutionary fame. Here the British massacred a Colonial outpost in October, 1778, and the site is marked by a stone monument.

"When I was seven years old, my father and uncle permitted me to accompany them on their Sunday expeditions and in time my own collection of Indian relics became extensive and varied.

"There were rumors that these farms contained buried treasures placed there during the Revolution. According to one story the Jillson Farm contained most of the buried treasure and this tale was told again and again by the old people in the vicinity.

"In the spring of 1890 my father, Arthur Jillson, was plowing the sloping meadow field. The plow-share struck something that turned it to one side. Having in mind the oft-repeated tales of buried treasures, my father uncovered the object. At first it seemed to be a rusted iron box but careful examination disclosed that it was a human skull. Further digging exposed a human skeleton, the remains of a man who had been buried in a sitting position. A clay pipe was also found in the grave.

"This skeleton was found in what we called a dark spot in the field. There were many such spots. The oldsters believed that these spots were the locations of Indian fires used to smoke shell fish, since there were many Indian shell piles in the vicinity. My father, however, had determined that the spots were caused by something in the ground affecting the growth of vegetation.

"Ultimately every dark spot yielded a skeleton, each in a single grave. Our meadow field had been an Indian burying ground, the only one of any considerable size in the Tuckerton area.

"There were thirty-two such spots in our meadow field and my father and uncle exhumed the thirty-two skeletons so located. This was done with great care. The soil being sandy and quite moist, the bones were soft and putty-like when first exposed but soon hardened in the air.

"The first skeleton found was the only one in which the body had been placed in a sitting position and it was assumed that it was the grave of a chief. All graves were along the slope of a hill and within an area about one hundred and fifty feet long and eighty feet wide.

"One grave was that of a squaw and her baby that had been buried beside her. The infant had a soapstone ornament at its neck, the only ornament found. All of the bodies had been buried at the same depth — about three feet — and the graves were not in a line or in rows.

"All, except the chief, were buried face up with the heads toward the west. There was nothing to indicate that the bodies had been wrapped for burial, nor were pottery, animal bones, beads or articles of any sort found except the clay pipe and soapstone ornament.

"My father and uncle carefully laid the bones out in the large second-floor room of the carriage house. Here they were permitted to harden. A rather amazing observation was made after several of the skeletons had been assembled and wired. Their heights varied from six feet four inches to six feet eight inches. Practically all were in that range.

"The skulls were all in perfect condition excepting one that had a small irregular hole in it. The foreheads were slanting and the cheek bones high. The teeth were perfect with the exception of the squaw. One skeleton was sent to a museum in Washington for identification and from there sent to another museum in the West.

"The Indian knives which we found in the course of our explorations were made of common local brownstone and some arrow heads were made of the same material. The spear heads were made of both yellow and brown flint stones not found in the Tuckerton area."

Mr. Jillson's narrative of the finding of the Indian burial ground on the family farm, and the above average height of the skeletons, seems to indicate that there might have been a pre-Lenni Lenape tribe in New Jersey as has been suggested by several Indian experts including Dr. Charles Abbott. The Lenni Lenape,, or Delawares, were rather medium in stature and one six feet tall was an exception.

The finds and specimens of Alfred and Arthur Jillson of Tuckerton are mentioned, and very favorably commented upon, in "The Mammals of Pennsylvania and New Jersey," by Samuel N. Rhoads, published in 1903.

CHAPTER IV

OLD "BARNIGATE" BEACH

Barnegat Inlet was named "Barnedegat," or "Breakers' Point," by the Dutch. Nearly all early spellings of the name of the Inlet, whether in writing or on maps, have an "a" or an "i" in place of the present day "e," some even ending the word with a final "e."

Samuel Groome, Surveyor-General of New Jersey, in 1683, wrote the Proprietors in London, "Barnegat I intend to see shortly after the season is fitting to go by land and water to it. I intend to go by water in a sloop and from thence come by land."

Gawen Lawrie, Deputy Governor of East Jersey and one of the Trustees for the Byllinger portion of West Jersey, on the 29th of the First Month (March), 1684, joined several others in writing as follows, "Barnagat, or Burning Hole, is said to be a very good place for fishing," and, "that it is good land with abundance of meadow lying to it." The name "Burning Hole" is often met with in old correspondence referring to Barnegat. Just what "Burning Hole" implied is still a mystery.

A Survey Map was made in 1769 for the Commissioners appointed to settle the boundary dispute between the Provinces of New York and New Jersey. This map was published in 1777 by Wm. Faden, Charing Cross, London.

Going northward from Cape May on Faden's Map of 1777 we find: One Mile Beach; Cold Springs Inlet; Two Mile Beach; Turtle Gut Inlet; Five Mile Beach; Hereford Inlet; Seven Mile Beach; Townsend's Inlet; Ludley's Beach; Customs Inlet; Peck's Beach; Great Egg Harbour; "Absecum" Inlet; an unnamed inlet; Brigantine Beach cut in two by Brigantine Inlet; Little Egg Harbour; Old "Barnigate" Beach; "Barnigate" Inlet; Island Beach; New Inlet and Squan Beach. Present day Barnegat Bay is shown as the Sound and Great Bay is designated as Flat Bay.

Comparing this to a recent map, and going in the same direction northward from Cape May, we find: One Mile Beach as Poverty Beach; Cold Springs Inlet as Cape May Harbor; Turtle Gut Inlet has been filled in thus joining Two Mile Beach and Five Mile Beach;

Ludley's Beach is Ludlum's Beach; Customs Inlet has become Corson's Inlet; Great Egg Harbour is Great Egg Inlet; "Absecun" has changed one letter to become Absecon; the unnamed inlet is now Absecon Inlet; the northern part of Brigantine Beach is Island Beach; Little Egg Harbour is Little Egg Inlet with Beach Haven Inlet, a new one, in place of the original Little Egg Harbour.

Old "Barnigate" Beach is now Long Beach and Island Beach goes as far as Bay Head. New Inlet has been filled in. Squan Beach has been absorbed by the all covering Island Beach which was recently acquired by the State of New Jersey from the Phipps Estate as a wild life refuge.

Long Beach, an island, for some seventy years prior to 1925, figuratively speaking, had a lighthouse at either end. Barnegat Light was at the north end. Little Egg Harbor or Sea Haven Light was on Short Beach, better known as Tucker's Beach, just across the lower inlet.

The great stretch of salt water between the mainland and Long Beach is continuous but has three divisional names: Barnegat, Manahawkin and Little Egg Harbor Bays. In 1942 several government agencies laid out and filled in a sand dyke extending into Barnegat Bay in a northerly direction for some three and one-half miles. This dyke is 210 feet wide at the base, 50 feet wide at the top and ten feet above average high water.

The Great Swamp of Long Beach apparently began at about where the railroad draw-bridge crossed the Bay from Milliard's to Barnegat City Junction, or about seven hundred feet north of the present causeway. The Swamp not only covered the present Surf City area but extended well above the present Harvey Cedars line.

The Ancient Cedars of New Jersey

Early maps and accounts of the northern part of Long Beach indicate that it was formerly several times its present width with the region heavily wooded. There were giant cedar and holly trees as well as many great hardwoods. The south side of Barnegat Inlet was particularly well timbered being the highest portion of Long Beach.

Henry Hudson's Log of the "Half Moon," under date of September 2, 1609, refers to Barnegat Bay as "a great lake of water, in length ten leagues, with drowned or sinking land." Special mention is made of the fine trees observed.

The terrific storm of September 3, 1821, still spoken of as "The Great September Gale," levelled many of the majestic trees of Long Beach. The hurricane of September, 1944, almost completely destroyed the remaining timber.

Around 1910 one of the large cedar trees in Harvey Cedars was blown down. A group of scientists from the University of Pennsylvania found that the trunk showed almost five hundred years of growth. Several old cedar trees still thrive south and west of the Harvey Cedars Hotel building.

About a century ago, Dr. Maurice Beesley, of Dennisville, made a study of the giant cedars of New Jersey. In a swamp near his home he found a cedar stump some six feet in diameter and personally counted one thousand and eighty rings of annual growth.

Whales and Whalers of Long Beach

The logs and journals of the early navigators from the 1600's onward comment on the great number of whales seen off the New Jersey coast. Whales are still there but in depleted numbers. The off-shore fishermen see them spouting and occasionally one may be seen by an observer outlooking at Barnegat Light.

Much has been written about whalers from New Haven and Long Island settling Cape May as early as 1640 thus creating the impression that whaling was an exclusively Cape May area industry in early New Jersey.

There was great whaling activity on Long Beach in the past. A few persons can still remember the mementoes of this in the whale bone fences and gateways that once surrounded houses in Surf City and High Point. While the whalers worked on Long Beach, and for many years thereafter, the beach was strewn with large whale bones bleached white by the sun.

The Long Beach whalers had their own method of operation which differed from the way the Cape May whalers worked. Long Beach whalers did not use large vessels nor did they seek whales far from the shore. Look-out towers were manned on the beach. When a whale was sighted the crew took their boat out through the surf and the chase began. If successful the whale was towed to the beach and there cut up and tryed.

Many old maps of Long Beach show a place about six miles below

Barnegat Inlet marked "Inmans," where one or more of the family of that name lived. Thomas F. Watson, in his "Annals" written in the 1820's, tells of a visit to Long Beach. He talked with old Stephen Inman, then over seventy and one of the family living at the place. He was surprised to find that Stephen and his family had never ceased to be whale catchers. They followed the occupation in February and March, generally taking two or three whales a season which averaged forty or fifty barrels of oil each.

Watson saw their lookout mast, their caldron and furnace for rendering the oil, their whale boat and many large whale bones bleaching on the beach. The famed and oft referred to "Inman Whaling Lookout Tower," according to Mrs. Emmor N. Lee, was on the beach in what is now Surf City, but almost to the Harvey Cedars line. The Inman dwelling was close by. This location is now well out to sea.

Records show that in the early 1800's a dead whale stranded on the Absecon bar, and was towed into the Inlet and beached by a group of Absecon men. They decided to process the whale and as they were so engaged they ran into difficulties. One of the Inmans from Great Swamp on Long Beach appeared and demanded one-half of the oil. He claimed that his boat had killed the whale and identified a broken harpoon in the carcass. The erstwhile whalemen of Absecon paid no attention to Inman, who then took the matter to court. The judge decided in favor of Inman and awarded not half of the oil, as he first claimed, but all of it and the whale bone as well.

Whaling along the New Jersey coast must have been extensive even at an early date as is indicated by the following advertisement from a 1780 newspaper:

> WANTED: Two experienced HARPONIERS in the whaling business, to enter the first day of November next, to whom good encouragement will be given by Henry Guest of New Brunswick.
>
> N.B.: None need apply without proper vouchers of their dexterity in the Business.

As practiced on Long Beach, whaling was a dangerous and arduous business. The endurance required of a crew was tremendous. Boats were launched through the surf on the coldest winter days. Then there was the backbreaking pull in pursuit of the whale, to be followed by a chilling wait as the harpooner sought the proper moment to make his thrust. Success or failure depended upon his skill.

The battle with the monster followed with an ever present danger from the line. Then there was the labor of hauling the line in so that a second harpoon might be thrown if possible. One small boat with its crew of five or six was pitted against a giant weighing as much as sixty tons.

If successful the captured carcass must be towed to the beach before it sank. Immediately the whale was cut up and rendered in order to secure the valuable oil. The average useful life of a whaler was about twelve years, with few caring to follow the trade because of the disabling injuries.

Whalers lived at the upper end of old High Point. When Harvey Cedars had a whaling station it is believed to have been manned by Norwegians. It is a matter of record that the open iron furnace and huge kettles used for rendering the blubber were stored the year round on upper Long Beach. They were there for many years after all whaling activity had ceased.

The Pirate of the New Jersey Coast Richard Worley

Much has been written about Barnegat pirates, buried treasure and devious practices used to lure unwary mariners onto Barnegat Shoals. Most of these stories are pure fiction. The shoals, inlets and pounding surf of the New Jersey coast were just as dangerously troublesome to the pirate navigators as they were to honest seamen.

But one particularly energetic pirate did strike terror along the seacoast of the Province of New Jersey during a career of six short weeks. Very little has been written about this unusual rogue and for some reason his name seldom appears in print.

Richard Worley began his brief career as a pirate in a small way in New York Bay in September of 1712, when he started off in a shallop with eight companions. The armament of this band consisted of six muskets; their supplies a cask of fresh water, some ship biscuit and a bit of smoked beef. No attention was paid to the small boat and nine men as it left the Bay and headed south.

Since Worley needed practically everything, as he proceeded down the New Jersey coast he boarded fishing vessels and small schooners, taking a little from each and exacting tribute. He did not attempt to seize the ships nor did he molest the crews. Working his way south, he entered Delaware Bay to the consternation of plantation owners on both shores.

He sighted a large comfortable sloop at anchor off Lewes, Delaware, which he and his crew boarded and seized. The sloop was very much to the pirate's liking and was well stocked with supplies and gear. The vessel was renamed "New York's Revenge" and with the shallop in tow the pirates set off.

News of the capture of the sloop reached Philadelphia and local ship-owners became alarmed. Word was sent to New York, Boston and other ports. New York ship-owners immediately sent out an expedition to destroy the pirate. Days were spent at sea without sighting him and the expedition returned.

The Governor of Pennsylvania, knowing that a British man-of-war, the "Phoenix," was at Sandy Hook, asked that this ship be sent to the Delaware Bay. The "Phoenix" sailed down the Jersey coast and into all coves and anchorages seeking Worley and his ship.

Worley cruised in and around Delaware Bay for some three weeks eluding capture. He was reported east, south, west and north, capturing ships and levying tribute. But while the "Phoenix" was searching for him he sailed toward the south where coastal commerce was still on the high seas and not being held in port in fear of him.

The Carolinas, and Charleston in particular, were active in combating pirates. They played a prominent part in having Edward Teach, better known as "Blackbeard," and Major Bonnet, known as "Captain Thomas," hanged. While Worley was sailing southward Bonnet was a prisoner in Charleston jail. The people of the town were fearful of a massed pirate attack to free the prisoner and sack the city.

When the report reached Charleston that a notorious pirate named "Moody" with two ships was outside the harbor collecting toll from incoming ships, it was believed that this was the beginning of the massing of a pirate fleet to attack the city. Led by Governor Johnson of South Carolina, the Charleston ship-owners acted promptly and a fleet of four armed merchant vessels was assembled. After a terrific battle the pirates were completely annihilated. Governor Johnson had gone out to capture "Moody" but was overjoyed to find he had really wiped out Worley and his crew.

The piratical career of Richard Worley thus ended in six weeks. In that time, however, he had terrorized New Jersey coastal shipping and had practically closed the ports of Philadelphia and New York.

CHAPTER V

THE GALLANT WORK OF THE VOLUNTEER LIFE BOAT CREWS

Owing to its geographical position, certain sea lanes have converged off Barnegat Inlet for centuries. Despite the latest scientific equipment on vessels and modern warning signals on Barnegat Lightship, the Barnegat Inlet Shoals and Long Beach still appear in the news with an occasional shipwreck.

Because of its location Long Beach took a tremendous toll of ships in the past. The shoals off shore were a continuous threat to the great number of coasters that had to pass them in going into America's two great ports, Philadelphia and New York. At one time both of these cities were virtually fed and fueled by these coastal schooners.

Volunteer life-saving crews functioned along the New Jersey coast, as well as along the entire Atlantic coast, before the establishment of the Federal Life Boat Service. These volunteer crews were staffed by local men often augmented by seamen from the mainland.

Much has been written about Captain Thomas Bond and the "House of Refuge" for survivors of wrecks that stood near his famed "Long Beach House" at the southern end of Long Beach. There was also one of these houses at Harvey Cedars and there are indications that there were others. There is no doubt that Captain Samuel Forman Perrine, Sr. was a member of a Long Beach life boat crew possibly as early as 1840.

In March of 1857, Captain Perrine, Sr., who was the first proprietor of the Harvey Cedars Hotel, was presented with a silver medal by "The Life Saving Benevolent Association," of New York, for the part he played in saving the lives of the crew of the British bark "Tasso," wrecked on the shoals of Barnegat Inlet, December 20, 1856.

Captain "Sammy" was then a member of the volunteer life-saving crew operating from the upper end of Long Beach and led by Captain Predmore of Great Swamp. This entire crew received medals from the British government for their bravery when the "Tasso" was wrecked.

The story of the tragedy and bravery of the "Tasso" rescue can best be gathered from the account in the "West Jerseyman," a newspaper printed in Camden. The item bears the date December 31, 1856.

"The Bark 'Tasso' and the immigrant ship 'New York' went ashore on the coast of Ocean County, near Wearstown, on the 20th inst., the last mentioned ship with 280 passengers and a crew numbering 23. Both vessels went ashore at the same time. The 'New York' lay a helpless wreck in the breakers, with her passengers in an almost perishing condition. The gallant New Jersey Shoremen were on hand, periling their own lives for the rescue of their despairing fellow creatures. Towards midnight the whole were landed, in a most deplorable condition, on a sterile, sandy beach, without food and destitute of shelter, save the scanty accommodations offered by the little life-saving station, which was barely sufficient to shelter a tenth of their number: men, women and children of all ages, huddled together for warmth and cowered upon the bare sand before the December blast. Here and there, a little driftwood was gleaned, or a few stray sticks gathered and kindled into a flame. These ghostly fires flickered faintly, but for a while rendering more apparent the utter desolation of the scene and the hour, and then went out. That was a dark and fearful night — if possible more dreadful than the previous one. How the wide Atlantic broke in angry boomings on the beach — how mothers drew their nestlings closer to their shrunken breasts and fathers cursed the fates that had lured them from their distant homes to famish on the foreign shore — we have no heart to tell. Children cried for bread, many of them had not eaten since Saturday but there was none to give. A single barrel of biscuit sent from the ship had scarce touched the beach before it disappeared. Such wretched beings we have never seen before, and hope never to behold again! Scantily clad, many of them in their hurry to escape from the ship had left the greater part of their clothing behind them. It is no wonder then that hungry, debilitated and hopeless, they sank on the sand in blank despair. Was this the end of all the privations, the toil which they had undergone to obtain the means of reaching America? Was this the realization of their dearest hopes and aspirations? Oh! We shall tell in what grim and undefined shapes arose those dreadful thoughts. Morning came, colder and more callous still — no shelter yet, and not a bit of food. Many of the sufferers were severely frost bitten during the night, and the prospect of bettering their condition seemed more distant than ever. Subsequently they were conveyed to the City of New York."

The "New York" went ashore on Island Beach, north of Barnegat Inlet. The "Tasso" struck the shoals south of the Inlet. News articles indicate that two members of the volunteer live-saving crew lost their lives in the rescue work.

The "West Jerseyman" of January 14, 1857, reported: "Wrecks on the Jersey Coast; — the whole number of wrecks on the Jersey Coast since the first of July, to the present time amounts to 48; persons on board 865; saved by Government apparatus 471; their own exertions and citizens' boats 314; whole number saved 785; lost 80 besides two surfmen who lost their lives in the attempt to save the crew of the 'Tasso'."

The "Ocean Emblem," a newspaper published in Toms River, New Jersey, by Lewis Shinn, reported: "The body of John F. Jones, one of the gallant Shoremen, was recovered on the 29th ult., and buried the following day, with a large attendance at his funeral. Rev. Joel Heywood preached the sermon and spoke in the highest terms of him. Over $1000.00 has been collected for his family."

The London Board of Trade awarded twenty pounds to the widow of John F. Jones. February 25, 1857, two months after the wreck of the "Tasso," it was reported that through the efforts of F. Merian, of New York, enough had been collected to purchase a house at Barnegat for the widow of Surfman Jones "who lost his life in his effort to save the wrecked crew of the British bark 'Tasso'."

Later the British Government awarded fifty pounds to the parents of John Parker, the other surfman who lost his life in the 'Tasso' rescue. Gold medals were awarded to Captains Howes and J. Predmore. Jeremiah Predmore was famous for his strong voice. It is said that he gave instructions to crews of grounded ships by shouting from the shore. His voice could be heard above the storms.

The committee having charge of the fund for the widow of Surfman Jones finally decided upon the purchase of a "snug farm on West Creek" for twelve hundred dollars.

By 1885 the cemetery facilities of the mainland were already taxed to take care of the ship-wrecked mariners who lost their lives on this coast. There were apparently no burials made on Long Beach and all of the bodies were taken to the mainland for interment.

Just how great a toll of shipping and life this coast took when several thousand schooners annually passed the location can be appreciated from an interview published in the "Long Beach News" of March 8, 1884, under the heading "Wrecks on This Beach": In conversation with ex-coroner W. A. Crane, concerning how many shipwrecked sailors were buried in the Baptist church-yard there (Manahawkin), the resting place of the unfortunate sailors of the English bark 'Ennina,' wrecked in the terrible storm of January 8, (1884) he said, "The church yard is over one hundred years old and probably as many bodies are laid away in it. Going back some years I remember the wreck of the 'Powhatan' from Bremen. She struck fast just opposite this place and went down with three hundred aboard. Of this number, 28 were buried in this yard by Isaac W. Peckworth, Justice of the Peace, some at Tuckerton and others at Waretown, West Creek and Barnegat. Some of the bodies were afterwards removed by friends. Twelve bodies were removed by R. F. Randolph and two by myself as Coroner; they being bodies of sailors belonging to the schooner 'Mary B. Snee' for New York, wrecked March 7, 1868. The villages mentioned also helped to bury the bodies of sailors who lost their lives in wrecks. They are situated on the mainland between Barnegat Inlet and Little Egg Harbor. The length of the Beach is more than twenty miles and the width of the Bay from two to seven miles. It is very difficult in bad weather, or ice as we have it now, to cross from the mainland to Long Beach. At this place the Bay is at its narrowest part and has a shoal bottom. In case of wrecks on the coast we can cross the Bay when others at points north and south of us cannot. By an understanding with parties living on the beach, in case of a wreck, word is sent here and I telegraph the authorities. I have reported in one week's time as many as seven wrecks on this beach. At one time I had to go all the way to New York to report since we had no telegraph then in this section of the State. The schooner 'David H. Toick' was wrecked in 1877 and three lives were lost. I buried them at West Creek. In conclusion I would state that this burying ground of the Baptist Church is filled up, it being small. Something should be done by our State, County or Township authorities to procure a piece of land from persons owning land near this churchyard and have it set apart and nicely fenced in. There all those cast away on the beach between the two named inlets could be buried, and there should also be kept a full description of the ship, etc., by the Coroners."

CHAPTER VI

BARNEGAT LIFE BOAT STATION

Barnegat Life Boat Station House was originally established during 1872. Life Saving Service records show that the first three Keepers of this Station were: Captain Samuel Forman Perrine, Jr., appointed November 22, 1872; Captain Joel H. Ridgway, appointed in February, 1876; and Cornelius Thompson, appointed September 29, 1899.

The Station's earliest extant log book is dated from December 1, 1875. The crew is listed in this log book as: Keeper, Samuel F. Perrine, Jr.; Surfmen: Stephen C. Imman, Joel H. Ridgway (afterwards Keeper); Solomon Soper, Holmes W. Russell, John L. Soper and William Imman.

In these early days the Keepers hired their own crews and the Stations were closed for the three summer months. Captain Samuel F. Perrine, Jr. was permitted to take four months off each summer so that he could skipper the schooner yacht "Sans Souci." He finally resigned to devote his full time to this yacht and was her captain until she was wrecked in 1906.

In the beginning Barnegat Life Boat Station was designated as Station No. 17 in the Fourth Life Saving District. Since Sandy Hook was Station No. 1 in this District, it means that Barnegat was the seventeenth along the New Jersey coast going southward. Bay Shore Station, just above Cape May Point was Station No. 40.

The Station Houses were roughly four miles apart and the surfmen walked the beach on regular patrols. The Half-Way Houses were about two miles above and below the Stations. Each mile of the seacoast was walked by an alert surfman every two hours.

About 1900 the Barnegat Life Saving Station was designated as Station No. 113 in the Fifth District, the No. 1 Station then being down east at the northerly end of the Maine coast. When the United States Coast Guard took over the Life Saving Service in 1915, the New Jersey Stations became part of the New York District of that branch of the Service.

The Life Saving Station at Barnegat City was rebuilt and enlarged

31

in 1884, and extensive improvements were made in 1906. The present Coast Guard Station at what is now known as Barnegat Light was erected in the early 1940's. The docks and boat-house of the present Barnegat Coast Guard Station are on the west side of Long Beach just south of Barnegat Inlet. Here several boats of various kinds for different purposes are ready for instant use.

The wreck reports filed by Captain Joel H. Ridgway while Keeper of the Barnegat Station give a vivid picture of the work of these men. We will select the fall and winter of 1885-1886 as a representative period. From November to April, Captain Ridgway filed seven wreck reports. The reports show that six of the vessels were saved — five of these being two masted schooners and a steamship of 1800 tons.

Captain Ridgway's crew at Barnegat Life Boat Station No. 17 in 1886 were Cornelius D. Thompson, Henry Reeves, John I. Soper, Solomon Soper, Alex Chandler, William Inman and Forman Perrine.

On November 10, 1885, the "Louisa B. Robinson," a two masted schooner of twenty-eight tons, hailing from Barnegat and owned by B. Predmore & Sons, stranded on Barnegat Shoals in a strong northwest wind. Captain Ridgway reported, "boarded vessel as soon as possible after striking, ran anchors with surf-boat and by use of sails succeeded in having her afloat in about one hour after boarding her when she proceeded into harbor, picked up anchor and cable with surf boat which had to be shipt, put it on board and returned to Station at about 11 a.m. (crew did not arrive at vessel until 9 a.m.)."

On January 7, 1886, the "J. and C. Merritt," a two masted schooner of thirty-five tons hailing from Somers Point, N. J., bound for Barnegat City with lumber, stranded on Barnegat Shoals one mile northeast from the Station. William Inman discovered the stranded vessel at 9 a.m. Here is Captain Ridgway's report, "boarded vessel as soon as possible after striking, ran anchors with surf boat and after working three tides succeeded in heaving her off at 9 a.m. January 8: piloted her in where she discharged her cargo without loss or damage."

The "Kraljarca," a six hundred ton bark of Fiume, Austria, stranded and sank on Barnegat Shoals, one mile east of Barnegat Station, in the early morning of February 11, 1886. She was bound for New York with a cargo of salt valued at twenty-five thousand dollars. There was an ebb tide with a heavy sea and a strong northeast wind with a thick fog.

The wreck was discovered by Captain Ridgway and John I. Soper, No. 1 Surfman of the Station. The Loveladies Station was notified and that crew came up the beach and helped man the Barnegat surf boat. Captain Ridgway's report tells what happened, "About 5.20 a.m. discovered a vessel on outside of the Shoals about a half mile from shore and about the same distance east of the Station. We immediately launched new Bebe surf-boat and started out to her assistance and when within about fifty yards found she had been abandoned, we then started to return to shore and when within about 400 yards took a very heavy set of seas which broke over our boat, filled her with water, turned her bottom up, all hands were thrown into the sea and John I. Soper, No. 1 Surfman, Solomon Soper, No. 2 Surfman and Samuel F. Perrine were drowned; bodies all recovered and sent home."

The Barnegat Life Boat Station crew members saved were Joel H. Ridgway, Cornelius D. Thompson, William Inman and Henry Reeves. Two of the surf boat crew were from the Loveladies Station.

The captain and the crew of the "Kraljarca" had taken to their boats and ran down the beach before the wind. They made a crash landing at Harvey Cedars with great casualties. The captain and the crew numbered fourteen — six were saved and eight lost. The fog was so thick that Captain Ridgway had no way of knowing from the shore that the vessel had been abandoned.

The Loveladies Station crew had brought their boat up the beach with them and when the Barnegat Station boat overturned those on the beach manned the Loveladies boat for the rescue. All were rescued except the three drowned. Henry Reeves was unconscious when brought ashore and William Inman was believed dead. Although permanently broken in health, William Inman served as postmaster at Barnegat on the mainland until his death.

On March 16, 1886, the two masted schooner "Carolina Augusta" of New York drifted ashore while fishing. This was about 8 a.m. She was floated at 6 p.m. without damage.

On March 22, 1886, the "Louis R. Robinson," bound for Hog Island, Virginia, stranded on Barnegat Shoals for the second time in four months. She was worked off with no damage save a broken steering gear.

The same day the two masted schooner "Farmer," thirty-two tons, was bound from Little Egg Harbor to New York with clams. She stranded on the Shoals due to a buoy being out of place. Captain Ridgway reported that his crew was working on the "Louis R. Robinson," which had struck an hour earlier. A heavy fog settled and the

"Farmer" was badly used by the seas. She was taken into the harbor and laid ashore where a leak was stopped and then continued on her way to New York.

The next wreck report of this series was that of the steamship "Eros," twelve hundred and eight tons, from Swansea bound for Philadelphia. Keeper Grim of the Loveladies Station called Captain Ridgway about 7 a.m., April 17, 1886, and reported that there was a steamship ashore south of his Station and asked the Barnegat crew for assistance. There was a thick fog, moderate northeast wind at high tide and heavy seas. The Barnegat crew started down the beach at once and arrived soon after the Loveladies crew had fired the shot line aboard.

Captain Ridgway made out at least fifty-two wreck reports during the period from September 18, 1883 to May 17, 1895. Most of the vessels were worked off the Shoals into deep water through hard work and expert seamanship. Some, however, were total wrecks.

Captain Ridgway's first wreck report, September 18, 1883, concerned the schooner yacht "Sans Souci" with Captain Sammy Perrine, Jr., as master. With the owner aboard fishing, the anchors would not hold and the yacht stranded in the Inlet in a strong north wind. The Barnegat surf boat was used to run anchors and the "Sans Souci" floated at high water.

From my study of Captain Ridgway's wreck reports, I find that the following ships were wrecked and sunk in the Barnegat Inlet vicinity between 1883 and 1895. "James Jones," two hundred and fifty ton schooner, loaded with soft coal, was run ashore in a sinking condition, and sank on northeast side of Barnegat Shoals on October 31, 1883. She was a total loss.

"Albertine Mayer," full rig brig of two hundred and sixty five tons from Rostock, Germany, carrying bagged sugar from Bahia, Brazil: stranded and sank on Barnegat Shoals, February 6, 1884. The vessel broke up in six hours after ship's crew were removed by Barnegat Life Saving crew.

"Deceiver," a small schooner from Somers Point, New Jersey, loaded with oysters stranded one mile north of the Station on April 29, 1884. Heavy seas pounded her and she soon broke up.

"Altavela," two master schooner loaded with stone for Washington, D. C., stranded on Barnegat Shoals, east northeast one mile from the Station on May 3, 1884. She soon began to break up.

"L. and A. Babcock," two hundred and fifty ton schooner loaded with coal was wrecked on Squan Beach, one mile north of Forked River Station, on June 26, 1884. Captain Ridgway had to round up a volunteer crew since the regular crew was off duty for the summer. The Barnegat surf boat was launched but because of the great wind and heavy seas did not reach the vessel until she had broken up. Five lives were lost.

"Guadelupe," of almost three thousand tons, with a crew of forty-nine and some eight passengers, loaded with a cargo of general merchandise and bound for Galveston, Texas, stranded and sank on Barnegat Shoals, one and one-half miles northeast of the Station on November 19, 1884. The Barnegat Life Boat Station crew and that of Loveladies Station made nineteen trips through the surf and all passengers and crew were saved.

"Lida Babcock," three masted schooner of two hundred and fifty tons, stranded on the north side of Barnegat Inlet in a snow storm, February 15, 1885. She quickly broke up in a heavy sea.

"Hayes," a small steamer bound for Toms River, was run on Barnegat Shoals in sinking condition on May 22, 1888. She broke up within three hours after stranding.

"J. W. Wendt," a ship of two hundred and fifty tons, from Bremerhaven, Germany, loaded with oil drums, stranded one mile north of Forked River Life Saving Station, on March 21, 1889, during a light snow storm. The ship was a total loss.

"James B. Johnson," two masted schooner of one hundred and fifty tons, hailing from Camden, New Jersey, and loaded with pine boards from North Carolina bound for New York, stranded one half mile south of Forked River Station, January 25, 1890. Vessel when boarded was full of water with no chance of saving her. Eight trips were made to convey her sails and rigging, of which she was stripped, to the beach.

"Dixie," a barge of one hundred and twenty tons, loaded with piles from Norfolk, Virginia, stranded and sank one half mile north of Barnegat Inlet, some two hundred yards from shore, April 20, 1893. Wreck was discovered by Albines Falkinburg, about 4.30 p.m. in heavy easterly rain storm. Barge "Magnolia" had stranded one mile farther north earlier. Both had broken loose from steamer towing them and were total losses.

I have been asked why there are no wrecks visible on Long Beach. My answer was that the wrecks are there both under water and covered with sand on the beach. When our summer home was built in 1927, the builder, in driving piles, ran into eighteen inches of sawed timber some eight feet below the surface of the dune. Several years ago the eroding tide uncovered and floated away a hundred feet long piece of wrecked schooner from our beach.

CHAPTER VII

LIFE BOAT STATIONS ON LONG BEACH

Prior to 1935 there were three Coast Guard Stations in commission on the upper half of Long Beach. Today the one establishment at Barnegat Light covers the area.

So much has been written about the name of the Life Boat Station below the Barnegat Station that I turned to the official records for the real facts. According to Lyle J. Holverstoll, of the National Archives and Records Service, the site of the original Loveladies Island Life Saving Station was first occupied by the Government for life saving purposes in 1871.

This was apparently under the authority given the Government by the Surveyor General of New Jersey, under date of February 14, 1849, to select any part of the unlocated beach (in New Jersey) for the purpose of erecting life saving station houses thereon and to occupy the sites selected without let or hindrance.

Lovelady Island in the Bay was the nearest distinguishing name for the site chosen for this particular Station. The change of name to Loveladies through the years was simply one of usage. The Island, shown on most old maps, was at the time much larger and quite close to the west shore line of the island of Long Beach. Thomas Lovelady, a well-to-do Englishman of Barnegat, on the mainland and one of its first settlers, used the island for his bird and duck shooting and bestowed his name on it.

Available records fail to disclose when the Loveladies Island Life Saving Station house was built but as the Station Log Book for 1873 is in existence the assumption is that it was built before that time.

Charles Cox, Sr., was the first Keeper of Loveladies. He was appointed November 22, 1872 and served until March 15, 1876, when Christopher J. Grimm was appointed. Some twenty years later James R. Cox was appointed Keeper in July of 1897.

The Log Book under date of December 1, 1873, lists the crew, in addition to Keeper Cox, as Surfmen Joseph K. Ridgway, Christopher Grimm, Jesse Perrine, Stephen Ridgway, Jesse Birdsall and Charles Cox, Jr.

38 UNDER BARNEGAT'S BEAM

The Loveladies Station was originally designated as No. 18 in the Fourth District, and after the turn of the century it was shown as No. 114 in the Fifth District, and so it remained until the absorption of the Life Saving Service into the Coast Guard in 1915.

The Station House was closed in 1917 when Keeper James R. Cox retired but was recommissioned in 1924 with Thomas L. Beers as Keeper. He was followed by Norris Cramer, Fred Bailey, Percy Bennett and Joseph Tilton. Keeper Tilton was the last Keeper of the Station while it had a full crew in 1923. He was then transferred to the Toms River Station and the Loveladies Station was placed on an auxiliary basis with Clarence D. Gant as Keeper and Russell Brown and Lester Mott as crew.

The closing entry in the last Log Book of Loveladies Station is dated Tuesday, December 17, 1935, and reads, "7.00 P.M. Inspected Station buildings, all in order. Station officially placed out of commission this date at 11.30 A.M. Clarence D. Gant, Keeper."

Around 1937 the Station House was opened and used for a year or more as an encampment for "National Youth." The Loveladies Station House is still on its original site, nicely painted and unchanged, and serves as a summer shop.

The "Long Beach Island Fishing Club" occupies a fine building some four miles south of the Loveladies Island Life Saving Station. This building was the Harvey Cedars Coast Guard Station No. 115 of the Fifth Life Saving District until decommissioned on May 21, 1938.

According to official records this Harvey Cedars Station was erected in 1901, just west of the old one which was no longer suitable for use. The old Station House was just east of the white fence that once enclosed the present site. The old station was sold and made into a cottage by Captain Howard Lukens of the "Atlantic House."

The first Harvey Cedars Life Boat Station, called the old Station, was built in 1872. It was No. 19 of the Fourth Life Saving District, No. 1 being at Sandy Hook. Charles Martin was appointed Keeper on March 15, 1873. He was followed by Benjamin F. Martin on March 15, 1876; Samuel F. Perrine, Jr. on September 5, 1879; John Kelly on October 4, 1883; Charles C. Crane on February 11, 1886; Hudson Gaskill on June 12, 1888; Alex C. Falkinburg on May 10, 1901; Harvey Smith in about 1910 and finally the last one — Calvin Hickman.

The earliest available list of surfmen at Harvey Cedars is for the 1879-1880 season. It is interesting because all of the men came from

LIFE BOAT STATIONS ON LONG BEACH

two mainland towns. The surfmen then were: Jack Kelly, later Keeper of this Station and also later Keeper of Barnegat Lighthouse, Vincent Inman, Mahlon Ridgway, Charles E. Cox, Henry Perrine and William Throckmorton, all of Barnegat on the mainland; and Isaac Crammer and William Bounds of Manahawkin.

There were very few buildings around the Harvey Cedars Life Saving Station some thirty-five or forty years ago. The "street" consisted of two wagon wheel tracks in the sand running from the boat room door on the north side of the Station House, toward the sea and winding through dunes on the beach.

The Crammer cottage was at the ocean end of this so-called "street" near a huge sand dune. The big storms of 1919 washed this dune away. Twice the cottage was moved back from the beach as the erosion continued. The hurricane of 1944 completely demolished the cottage.

There was also a large two-family house known as the Ridgway cottage. This too was badly damaged by the 1944 hurricane but was moved down the Bay shore and repaired. It still stands there.

The Conrad cottage adjoined the Ridgway place. This was so badly battered by the 1944 storm that what remained was torn down. The railroad station at Harvey Cedars Life Saving Station was known as "Conrad's." The owner of the cottage had erected a small platform above the meadow grass.

Captain Alex Falkinburg, of Harvey Cedars Station, was from Tuckerton. He was a short, slender, mild-mannered man and a fine seaman. He was Keeper of the Station for more than fifteen years.

Captain Harvey Smith also came from Tuckerton. He was a large man with a waxed moustache and had been quarter-master on the American cup defender "Columbia." He had two hobbies — a very fine sneak-box he had built and he whittled decoy ducks.

Captain Calvin Hickman was a Port Republic man. He was a seaman of wide experience and had been skipper on the old steam, coal burning Menhaden boats working out of Crab Island, above Atlantic City, and Lewes, Delaware.

The crew of the Harvey Cedars Life Saving Station consisted of a Keeper, usually called the Captain, and seven surfmen. Before World War I the crew members were nearly all local men, either baymen or seamen, from Barnegat, Tuckerton or Manahawkin.

Once each week, weather permitting, the boat was hauled to the beach, launched through the surf, rowed from shore and turned over.

It was then righted and brought back. A record was kept of the time required to accomplish this drill.

There were no pensions in those days for men injured in the line of duty. When a surfman was unable to pass a physical examination he was through. Several men of the Harvey Cedars Station had been injured as well as men from other Stations, but they had no redress.

The bark "Fortuna," hailing from Trapani, Italy, in ballast, stranded on the beach, a half mile north of Ship Bottom Life Saving Station, on January 18, 1910. The weather was thick and stormy and the tide very high. She stranded in an upright position.

On board were the Captain, thirteen seamen, four passengers — the Captain's wife and three children — one a very young baby. All were saved by the Ship Bottom and Harvey Cedars Life Saving crews, as well as several young pigs and the ship's cat. On January 22, 1910, the "Fortuna" heeled over with her rigging dangling.

Pictures of the "Fortuna" piled up on the beach near Surf City appeared on many calendars the next year. But accounts accompanying the pictures were confusing. I discovered the cause of this confusion when I received copies of the wreck reports of the Ocean City and Wick Island Life Saving Stations, both in Maryland, from the National Archives. A ship of the same name, the "Fortuna," had stranded and sunk on the Maryland shore some hundred and twenty-five miles south of Surf City, on December 4, 1911.

The four-masted schooner "Cecil B. Stewart" struck the beach in front of the Francis Fenimore house at Harvey Cedars on February 17, 1927. The weather was heavy. Her cargo of railroad ties shifted and she split in half from stem to stern. The wreck drifted up the beach and finally came to rest at Twenty-first Street, Barnegat City. Two heavy timbers from this wreck make a fine mantel in our home in Barnegat Light.

After this wreck the insurance adjusters went up and down the beach in trucks, paying fifty cents each for railroad ties carried out to the road. Hard as the work was, some of the salvagers earned more than a hundred dollars a day since the cargo consisted of thousands of ties. One Barnegat Light man told me that he had salvaged more than sixteen hundred ties in a week.

During the years the wreck sank into the sand and was completely covered. In 1955 the erosion uncovered the wreck and all that remained of this once sizeable vessel finally floated down the beach.

CHAPTER VIII

"OLD BARNEY"
BARNEGAT LIGHTHOUSE

It is very probable that prior to the Government erecting a lighthouse at the north point of Long Beach in 1835, and even as far back as pre-Revolutionary times, the dwellers on the beach on the south side of Barnegat Inlet hoisted lighted lanterns to the tops of tall spars or trees to assist masters of incoming coastal vessels through the Inlet.

The first lighthouse on the New Jersey coast was established at Sandy Hook and was apparently put in service June 18, 1764. Prosperous New York merchants, in order to assist their vessels in making the harbor, raised funds by lottery and contribution, to build and maintain a white stone tower showing a white light at night. The tower was built at Sandy Hook and is still in use.

During the Revolution, the Sandy Hook Lighthouse was an ever present threat and menace to the home life and very existence of the Colonists. It was occupied by the British who fortified it in such a manner that it was known as "Lighthouse Fort" and "Refugee Town." From here Tory refugees and Royalists made many swift and cruel raids on their fellow Jerseymen.

Captain John Conover of the Continental Army, in 1776, was ordered to capture the place and end these depredations. He made a successful foray with a small company of men and the lighthouse apparatus was shot away and destroyed to prevent the British from using the beacon.

When the Sandy Hook Lighthouse was re-established the greed of the New York merchant-owners compelled the United States Government to take over the Light and end the merchant-monopoly. These men had insisted upon a heavy toll on each unit of tonnage entering the harbor whether daily market boats bringing food and fuel for the inhabitants of New York or foreign trade.

While Sandy Hook Lighthouse was the first on the New Jersey coast, it was not the first lighthouse on the Atlantic coast. "Lighthouses of the World," (1873) states that the following lighthouses were established in the years indicated: Brant Point, Mass., 1759; Sandy Hook,

N. J., 1762; Plymouth, Mass., 1769; Boston and Nantucket, Mass., 1784; Portland Harbor, Maine, 1799; Cape Henry, Virginia, 1791; Cape Henlopen, Delaware, 1792; Tybee Island, Georgia, 1793; Beaver Tail, Rhode Island, 1793; Montauk Point, N. Y., 1795; Cape Cod Highlands and Baker's Island, both in Massachusetts, 1797; Eaton's Neck, Connecticut and Cape Hatteras, North Carolina, 1798.

This list differs considerably from the usually accepted list of the first five lighthouses established on the Atlantic coast: Boston, Mass., 1716; Brant Point, Mass., 1746; Beavertail, Rhode Island, 1749; New London, Connecticut, 1760 and Sandy Hook, N. J., 1764.

The importance of having a beacon at the north point of Long Beach can be appreciated when it is remembered that before the Civil War hundreds of small schooners, generally built on the mainland and commonly called "coasters," plied the Atlantic coast. Their home ports were usually mainland towns with their crews from the same locality.

These "coasters" carried on a tremendous trade between the shore area and the large cities, especially in supplying Philadelphia and New York with lumber, charcoal, cord wood, manufactured goods and food stuffs. On their return trips they brought back to villages the many items that could not be made locally as well as merchandise for the shop keepers.

Nine lighthouses were established along the New Jersey coast to enable vessels to navigate the area safely and enter the inlets and bays for protection in times of storms. These lighthouses were:

1. Sandy Hook Light, about a mile south of Sandy Hook, established in 1764 as before mentioned.

2. Cape May Light, on the northeastern side of the entrance to Delaware Bay, established in 1823.

3. Highland Lights, on eastern shore of Navesink, established in 1828 on a hill side almost 250 feet above sea-level.

4. Barnegat Light, on south side of Barnegat Inlet, established in 1835.

5. Sandy Hook, East Beacon, at northern point of Sandy Hook, established in 1842.

6. Sandy Hook, West Beacon, on Bay side, established same year as above.

7. Little Egg Harbor Light, on Short Beach near entrance Little Egg Harbor, established 1848.

8. Absecon Light, now in Atlantic City, established 1854.
9. Hereford Light, north of Five Mile Beach, established 1874.

The First Barnegat Light

On June 30th, 1834, the Congress of the United States authorized the erection of a lighthouse at the north end of Long Beach and appropriated six thousand dollars for the purpose. Work was begun at once on a brick tower forty feet high, placed on a sand hill some hundred yards from the inside beach. There was a fixed white light with a focal plane of fifty-four feet above mean high water.

The newly established Barnegat Lighthouse was apparently put in commission just before the appointment of Henry V. Low, as Keeper, on August 3rd, 1835. He served until his death March 12th, 1838. His assistant-keeper was evidently a relative, for John H. Low was then appointed Keeper on March 31st, 1838.

Henry V. Low was a man of great courage. When the brig "Morgania," a pest ship with several cases of the dread small-pox aboard, piled up on the Barnegat Shoals early in 1837, the survivors, including the master of the ill fated ship, Captain Libby, were taken in by Keeper Low and nursed back to health.

Garret G. Herring was appointed Keeper on April 6, 1839. He was succeeded by Jeremiah Sprague, appointed June 15th, 1841. Sprague was succeeded by John Allen, appointed March 12th, 1846. John Warren followed Allen, being appointed November 12th, 1849, and he was followed by Charles Collins, appointed April 4, 1851. John N. Townsend did a short shift as Keeper from June 9, 1853 to May 31, 1854. Then came James Fuller, originally a Vermonter, who was appointed from New Jersey.

Apart from the fact that inspection reports stated that this original Barnegat Lighthouse was "built of inferior materials," complaints about the visibility of the light were continuous. Just when ten Argand lamps and reflectors were installed is uncertain, but we do have a record of larger reflectors being installed to increase the intensity of the light. Navigators continued to complain about the inadequacy of the light.

Lieutenant David D. Porter, U.S.N., commanding the United States Mail Steamer "Georgia," in July, 1851, wrote, "The first in order of our coast is Barnegat Light, much improved in late years by the substitution of large reflectors in place of the small ones formerly used, yet it is a very dull light."

Captain H. K. Davenport, U.S.N., commander of the United States Mail Steamer "Cherokee," reported on May 18th, 1852, "Barnegat Light is but an indifferent one, is frequently mistaken for a vessel."

The complaints produced some results. Changes were at least tried and a report states, "Since July 1st, 1854, lenses have been introduced in this District as follows: at Barnegat, a 4th order of 360 degrees to replace 10 Argand lamps and reflectors." This was a Fresnel apparatus, of the fourth order, deemed powerful enough for the limited range of this Light, which was ten miles at most.

The light apparatus was taken out of the original brick tower, when it became endangered, and installed at the top of a temporary wooden tower, around June, 1857, and was used there until the present Barnegat Lighthouse was commissioned.

The first Barnegat Lighthouse and the temporary tower were staffed by a Keeper and an assistant-keeper. The Department maintained a Keeper's house. It is impossible now to ascertain where this was located and whether it contained quarters for the assistant-keeper.

Erosion caused the original Barnegat Lighthouse tower to topple into the sea and evidently the Keeper's cottage was destroyed at the same time. There is an inference in the reports that quarters for the Keeper were built into the base of the temporary wooden tower.

The official reports simply state that the original brick tower fell in 1857, but an account in "The West Jerseyman," of November 11, 1857, stated, "The Lighthouse at Barnegat, Monmouth County, fell on the 2nd inst. Its condition promised this result for some time and the temporary one in its place has just been completed."

General George Gordon Meade and the Barnegat Light

General George Gordon Meade (1815-1872), who will always be remembered for his part in the Battle of Gettysburg, in 1863, had a great deal to do with the planning and building of the present Barnegat Lighthouse. As Lieutenant Geo. G. Meade, Topographical Engineers, he was attached to the Engineer's Office, Fourth Lighthouse District, in Philadelphia, almost continuously from 1842 to 1856.

"OLD BARNEY" BARNEGAT LIGHTHOUSE

He signed the report dated September 20th, 1855, submitted to the Lighthouse Board, Treasury Department. This report contained the specifications and recommendations pertaining to the Lighthouse at Barnegat. Part of this report states, "I visited the Barnegat Lighthouse in company with the district inspector, and now have the honor to lay before the Board the following report based on this examination. The tower at Barnegat is itself only forty feet high. It was recently furnished with a Fresnel apparatus, in the fourth order, which is sufficiently powerful for this limited range. The tower was found to be in very bad condition, originally built of inferior materials, the mortar had decayed and fallen out, so that in many places the bricks are without mortar, and settling in consequence, there was about ten feet below the lantern, a bulging out of the wall on the outside and in some places the bricks had fallen out. A new tower being absolutely necessary, in presenting plans for same, it is proper I should present the considerations which have governed me in the design, in order to justify the amount asked for construction. The light at Barnegat is emphatically a seacoast light, and should be of the first class. Its real purpose is to make known their positions to mariners from over the seas, who first make land in this vicinity. A glance at the map will show its great importance in this respect."

Later in the report Meade referred to the fact that the Keeper of the Light made a record of the number of large vessels in sight from his Station during daylight for the first three-quarters of the year. They totalled almost twelve hundred square rigged vessels and steamers, to which should be added the immense coasting trade of fore-and-aft vessels. It was estimated that as many again were in the vicinity at night.

In a later report Meade broke down the figures of the Keeper as to the number of vessels passing the Light during daylight hours as: ships 313, brigs 524, steamships 247. The great majority of these ships took their pilots on off Barnegat.

Meade submitted two plans; No. 1: for a first class light, the tower to be 150 feet high at an estimated cost of $45,155.75; No. 2: for a second class light requiring a tower of 80 feet and an estimated cost of a little over $30,000. The second plan was rejected.

The Present Barnegat Lighthouse

On August 18th, 1856, the Congress of the United States authorized the erection of a first-class Lighthouse at Barnegat to replace the one that was crumbling into ruins. The sum of $45,000 was appropriated for the work.

The 150 foot tower was to be placed some 75 feet back from the old tower. The foundations were to be of granite sunk ten feet below the surface. The superstructure was to be of brick, laid in cement, 27 feet in diameter at the base and 15 feet at the top. This gave a slope, inside and out, of one-half inch to the foot. A brick cylinder was to be built in the interior, nine inches thick and ten feet six inches in diameter in the clear, forming the well for an iron stairway.

These specifications seem to put an end to a legend that has persisted on Long Beach and the mainland that the Lighthouse is built on a foundation of teak wood piling. The specifications read: "the foundation is of granite sunk ten feet below the surface."

The calculated coefficient of stability was nine. That is, the Lighthouse was built nine times stronger than required to resist the maximum force of the wind. Despite this the tower did sway in the wind. One of the favorite pastimes of the old timers was to have a newcomer carry a full bucket of water to the lantern platform and then watch the consternation when a third of the water spilled over the sides of the bucket as the platform swayed.

Inside the tower a spiral iron stairway of two hundred and seventeen steps ascended to the lantern platform. There were landings at each of the four windows in the tower wall and each window marked a point of the compass. The narrow center end of each cast-iron step was attached to, or formed a part of, the large supporting iron pipe running up the center of the tower. This center pipe housed the cords and heavy weights that caused the great lens to slowly revolve.

"Winding up the lens" was a great task. The weights weighed more than 150 pounds and the cords were more than one hundred feet long. It was necessary to wind this mechanism between sunset and sunrise so that ten seconds of darkness would be maintained accurately as the lens revolved. While one keeper wound up the mechanism another would turn the lens by hand in order to maintain the proper interval.

The new Lighthouse tower at Barnegat, the one now standing, was completed late in 1858. The lens and lamp were of French make and cost $15,000 in addition to the cost of building the tower.

The huge gleaming lens was made up of some 1024 rectangular prisms, each several inches wide and some ten inches long, individually mounted in a bronze frame, thus forming 24 bull's eye lenses. The apparatus weighed five tons and was almost fifteen feet high, yet it was so finely balanced on ball bearings that it could be rotated with the slightest pressure. When the Lighthouse was finally decommissioned this lamp was taken to the Tompkinsville Lighthouse Depot on Staten Island.

The great beam of light from this lamp when it was in full operation seemed to have a particular attraction for migrating birds and it was necessary to protect the lamp with a heavy mesh screen. Each morning in fall and spring there would be a great number of killed and injured wild geese, brant, ducks and other night flying birds around the base of the tower.

Barnegat Light, the second tallest lighthouse tower in the United States, was commissioned at sunset, January 1st, 1859. This Station remained a light of the first class until about August 15th, 1927, when the Barnegat Lightship was established some eight miles at sea off Barnegat Shoals. When the Lightship took over, Barnegat Light was reduced from 80,000 candle-power to 11,000. The beam of Barnegat Light was darkened in 1943 as a precautionary war measure and so remained for about seven years.

The land on which Barnegat Lighthouse stands, a parcel of about two acres, was deeded to the State of New Jersey by the Federal Government on May 8, 1926, the Coast Guard reserving the right to maintain an automatic light in the tower, which it did until January, 1944.

As part of the celebration of the One Hundredth Anniversary of the establishment of Ocean County, observed on February 15, 1950, a smoll token light was turned on by Mayor John H. Heitsenroder, of Barnegat Light. This token light was masked from the sea.

The story of Barnegat Lighthouse is one of a continuous struggle against the encroachment of the sea. Excerpts from various official reports give a picture of this:

1866 — "beach near Lighthouse has been washed away, brushwood jettees (sic) being built along beach on the inside bay."

1867 — "storms and ice destroyed most of the work done last season

... about 200 tons of rough quarry stones deposited on jettees ... plank platform between Keeper's dwelling and the tower renewed and fence around building repaired."

1868 — "331 tons of stone placed on jettees ... storms and running ice damaged jettees ... 630 tons of stone deposited on September 30 ... tower and oil house washed with brick colored cement from top half-way down, lower half white washed; two panes of heavy glass for the lantern have been supplied, also drip buckets for oil drips.

1869 — "in 1868, 1220 tons of stone were deposited along the beach and in the jetties (first time spelled with 'I') and 16 new jetties have been built since that time, over 620 tons of stone deposited along the beach, on pier and in ballasting the brush wood jetties. The present high-water line is where low-water line was in 1867.

The wooden lining and part of the watch-room having been injured by fire last year, repaired and covered with sheet zinc to prevent recurrence of the accident. Repairs made to insure the regular and uniform movements of the revolutions of the illuminating apparatus, glazing of the lantern attended to, new pump, with check valve, put in assistant keeper's cistern; everything at this time is in good order and the light well kept."

1871 — "part of riprapping having slidden into deep water, three new jetties built, requiring 993 tons of stone."

1874 — "the changes of the position of the sand hills, north of the dwelling, are very marked. The store house is covered with drifting sand."

1875 — "during the very cold weather of last winter, the mechanical lamps which have been in use at this station for many years became unserviceable, and their place was supplied by new lamps of the Funck pattern; electric bells for calling the relief-keeper have also been placed in position."

1877 — "since 1839, the date of the first survey obtainable, the abrasion of the shoreline of this section has been constantly going on; the high-water mark having receded in this time nearly half a mile, caused by the ebb tide current from the bay which hugs the shore in front of the Lighthouse ... there is perhaps no more useful light on our coast and preservation of this site is necessary, at least for a time; appropriations of $10,000 for the cost of protecting works is recommended."

1878 — "the wearing away of the shore-line on the bay is increasing;

the sand has piled around the base of the tower to a considerable height and the lower part of the tower will be buried; it may be necessary to raise the dwellings and make an entrance to the tower through an upper window. The top of the pedestal has been much cut, the chariot so much worn that for several years past the revolutions of the lens have been irregular. A new chariot and clock-work have been made and are now being placed in position."

1880 — "a new store house has been built for fuel, etc., and the platform between the dwelling and the tower raised above the drifting sand. The tower and oil room have been cement washed on the outside, the iron stairway and the tower windows and the tin roof of the oil house and the room and work-room painted. Unless the abrasion of the beach can be entirely checked, the ultimate destruction of the Lighthouse building is inevitable. There is still $9,000 of the appropriation of $10,000 approved June 20, 1878, for the protection of the site, in the Treasury."

1883 — "a new plank walk was laid from the dwelling to the landing, new iron water conductors were placed where necessary. Porcelain lined cucumber pumps were put in the cisterns, a drive-well with an iron pump was set up in the kitchen shed, the boundaries of the site were marked with monuments. Arrangements were made to substitute mineral oil for the lard oil now in use."

1887 — "surveys show that the shore-line is rapidly receding and that means would have to be devised to prevent its continued cutting away, in order to insure the safety of the lighthouse."

1888 — "a new ground connection was furnished to the lightning conductor."

1891 — "a detached brick oil house was built. The second assistant keeper has no quarters except one room he occupies in the quarters of the first assistant keeper. Another dwelling should be erected at this station so that the keepers can live with their families in at least as much comfort as can be had by skilled workmen in cities."

1893 — "alterations to the dwelling, to give suitable and sufficient accommodations for the keepers, were begun in April."

1894 — "the alterations and remodeling of the keeper's dwelling in progress at the close of last fiscal year, were completed."

1899 — "a flagstaff was erected, a telephone installed, and a set of signal flags, etc., furnished."

The Keepers

James Fuller was the last Keeper of the original Barnegat Lighthouse and only Keeper of the temporary frame tower erected in 1857 when the sea endangered the original Light. He was appointed Keeper of the new Barnegat Lighthouse on January 6th, 1859.

The only record of his assistants that I have been able to locate states, "At the time James Fuller was appointed Keeper of the new Barnegat Lighthouse in January, 1859, James Cook was first assistant Keeper and George F. Fuller was second assistant."

Hiram M. Horner was second Keeper of the Lighthouse, being appointed on September 25th, 1861. He was followed by A. B. Brown, whose appointment was dated December 17th, 1862.

John Kelly followed Brown, his appointment being dated October 23rd, 1866. He, in turn, was followed by William C. Yates, a Pennsylvanian, November 25th, 1873. Yates was transferred to another station on October 2nd, 1875, and was succeeded by Joshua H. Reeves, who had served as assistant Keeper at Barnegat from May 6th, 1873. Reeves was transferred to Ludlum Beach Light Station on October 2nd, 1885 and served there until he retired on August 6th, 1946.

Another Pennsylvanian, Captain Thomas Bills, was appointed Keeper of Barnegat Light on October 13th, 1885, a position he held until October 1st, 1896, when he was transferred to Absecon Light Station, where he remained until his death on October 22nd, 1914. Captain Bills was followed by Abram C. Wolf, who served but a few months from September 12th, 1896 to December of the same year.

The next Keeper of Barnegat Light is still remembered by some residents of Long Beach. He was Captain William T. Woodmansee, generally called "Captain Tom" by those who knew him. He served as either first or second assistant keeper from March, 1883, to December 10th, 1886, when he was appointed Keeper and served in that position until his death on April 9th, 1915.

I am indebted to Mrs. Minnie D. Kelley and Mr. Percy B. Lovell for the information that for a time Captain Tom's first assistant keeper was Clarence H. Crammer and his second assistant keeper was Samuel Soper.

Clarence H. Crammer was appointed Keeper on April 10th, 1915. The initial "H" in his name stands for "Hazelton," a name of long standing and good repute in the Barnegat-Manahawkin area. He had served as first and second assistant keeper since May 8, 1883, and retired as Keeper September 30th, 1926. His whole long career in the Lighthouse Service was spent at one Station — Barnegat.

Andrew E. Applegate was actually the last Keeper of Barnegat Lighthouse. His appointment was dated October 2nd, 1926, but he had many years of service as assistant keeper. When the Government placed the Barnegat Lightship off shore, the candle-power of Barnegat Light was reduced as was its status from a watched light to an unwatched (automatic) light on August 15th, 1927.

As of August 23rd, 1927, Keeper Applegate's classification was changed to Lamplighter. He was drowned while fishing at sea on September 14th, 1928. His widow, Mrs. Bertha Applegate, conducted the general store and post office at Barnegat City for many years prior to 1950, in the building near the Lighthouse known as the Butterworth Post Office Building, now closed.

Robert E. Applegate, son of the above Keeper, was appointed Lamplighter on September 15th, 1928. The last Lamplighter at this Station was William A. Rothas, appointed March 1st, 1932. He served until Barnegat Lighthouse Station was darkened on March 31st, 1940.

This list of Keepers of Barnegat Lighthouse was secured by the help of many Government agencies, in several cities, and years were spent in collecting and checking the data.

These men performed a valiant service. There was at least one Keeper on duty on the lantern platform at all times when the light was in operation. The proper interval of the light had to be maintained for identification by mariners. When extremely cold weather caused the oil to congeal, it had to be warmed. When high winds swayed the tower so that the mechanical apparatus would not function it was necessary to operate the lens manually.

All of the oil for the lamp had to be carried up those two hundred and seventeen steps. Many still remember how a five gallon can of oil was always kept at the bottom of the steps so that anyone going to the top might carry it along and do double duty.

The Keeper's Dwelling at Barnegat Lighthouse was not enlarged until the early 1890's so that it would adequately house the families of the Keeper and his two assistants. September 14th, 1893, was moving day into the enlarged quarters. This house contained some twenty rooms and three baths, with plenty of porches and five large brick chimneys. It was located quite close to the tower on the ocean side, and is generally shown in pictures of Barnegat Lighthouse taken prior to 1920.

Erosion by the sea during the stormy winter of 1919-1920 made the Keeper's Dwelling untenable. It was sold for a pittance as it stood. A few items such as the heating plant were salvaged and the sea battered down what was left. Captain Axel Jacobson said to me, "When I came here in April, 1920, all that was left was bricks in the cellar covered by water." Captain John Larson, who skippered the dragger "Mary Jane," told me that in the spring of 1920 his father said to him, "John, we tie no more rocks in the lobster pots, we tie in bricks, plenty of these are now on the beach." The brick chimneys and cellar walls of the Keeper's Dwelling of Barnegat Lighthouse were put to use in this manner.

BAYARD RANDOLPH KRAFT

Photograph by Nathaniel R. Ewan.

Barnegat Lighthouse and Keepers' dwellings in September, 1919. The families of the Keeper and two Assistant-Keepers lived in this twenty room house. A few weeks after the photograph was taken, pounding seas made the buildings untenable; sold for a pittance, some materials were salvaged. The surging seas swept in and by April, 1920, the house was gone, the cellar walls were awash. Today the waters of Bay and Ocean lap at the very door of the Lighthouse.

Photograph by Nathaniel R. Ewan.

Barnegat Pier railroad station in 1915, said to be the only railroad station in the middle of a long bridge.

Photograph by Nathaniel R. Ewan.

The former home of "Indian Ann" Roberts, at Dingletown, N. J. This dwelling was built around 1882 by Indian Ann and was owned in 1946 when the photograph was taken, by George Cromwell, whose Grandmother was a Reservation Indian.

Photograph by Nathaniel R. Ewan.

Captain Thomas Bond's famous 'Long Beach House", below Beach Haven, just a few months before it was torn down in 1908.

The "new" house of the PEAHALA CLUB on the beach at Peahala, Long Beach. The building in the rear is the old club house used for storage purposes when the photograph was taken in 1903.

The enlarged Harvey Cedars Hotel. Photograph taken by the author in 1923 from a makeshift boardwalk to the railroad station. The narrow walk was built to take the place of a section of the original walk which was as wide as the part of the walk where the row boats are. Understand ice and storm tides raised up and carried away a part of the original walk. The Philadelphia Y.W.C.A. ran the hotel as Camp Whelen at this time.

Photograph courtesy Delaware State Archives, Hall of Records, Dover, Delaware.

Batsto bog iron fire-back in the Ridgely homestead, on the Green, Dover, Delaware. This is the only one of this design ever seen by the author; the several seen have a small oak tree in the center with either a bird or squirrel in the tree and a hunter on the ground.

57

Courtesy Mrs. Joseph E. Roberts.

The famed figurehead, west of the old Harvey Cedars Hotel porch in 1902. For no reason now know, she was called "Hannah" by the Hotel guests. The fate of the figure-head is unknown. The young ladies sailed down from High Point to have their picture taken with the wooden figure.

The Italian Barque "FORTUNA" came ashore on January 18, 1910, in an upright position at Surf City and on the 22nd, rolled over on her beams end. The hull, spars and most of the rigging were made of steel. The metal was salvaged, cut into small pieces, freight car loads were shipped to American steel mills. Photographs of this wreck were used on thousands of calendars for several years. This is a bow view.

Courtesy J. Lawrence Fenimore.

Engine No. 2 of Manahawkin & Long Beach Transportation Company, nick-named the "Tar Pot" because it smoked so badly outside the engine house at Harvey Cedars in 1906; this engine was too large to get inside the engine-house which was built for the "Yellow Jacket."

Courtesy Nathaniel R. Ewan.

The "DUMMY", built at Baldwin Locomotive Works, Philadelphia for summer season 1893, after a bit of service. The smoke stack raised for better draft, scrape board placed in front of the drive wheel, no screens. According to Alex H. Inman who worked on the railroad from 1904 to 1909, the engineer in the doorway is George Morton Crane, others claim it is Arch Pharo and the last name of the man at the window was Bishop.

Courtesy Miss Marguerite Robinson.

ASHLEY HOUSE, Barnegat City in 1887. The abandoned "Herring—Ashley—Kinsey House" between the Lighthouse and the old Butterworth Post Office Building a few months before it was torn down.

Photograph courtesy J. Lawrence Fenimore.

Snow and the Old Harvey Cedars Hotel on March 21, 1892. The oldest picture of the old hotel that the author could obtain; although there are several older paintings. Picture apparently taken from the roof of the oyster house.

Courtesy J. H. Perrine.

Captain Samuel Forman Perrine Jr., of Barnegat on the mainland, at the wheel of the schooner-yacht "Sans Souci" in the early 1890's. Captain Perrine skippered her from the time she was launched in 1875 until she was abandoned in 1906.

U.S. Coast Guard Photo.

Barnegat Lightship

CHAPTER IX

EARLY BOARDING HOUSES ON LONG BEACH ISLAND

A boarding house to accommodate visitors from the mainland was established on the island of Long Beach before the Revolution. In 1765, Reuben Tucker, of Orange County, New York, purchased a small portion of lower Long Beach and built a house which was enlarged from time to time. Not only was this a home for him and his family, but he also took in boarders.

In 1800 storms cut a new inlet through the lower end of the Island separating the Tucker land from the rest of the Island. This then became known as Short Beach or more familiarly "Tucker's Beach." The Tucker family entertained visitors from the mainland and "Tucker's Beach" became quite popular.

Watson, the Philadelphia Annalist, visited "Tucker's" in the early 1820's and wrote, "The house at Tucker's Beach is a cluster of three houses built at different times. The original house of the celebrated Mother Tucker is a one-story house with hipped roof and a front piazza."

Surf City is now just a bit above the center of Long Beach Island and is the location referred to in early accounts as Great Swamp. A large boarding house was erected there in 1822 and the place name was then changed to that of the house — 'Mansion of Health.'

The same Watson mentioned that in 1821-1822 he visited the "Philadelphia Company House" on Long Beach. This was located several miles below the present Beach Haven and was then being run by Captain Joseph Horner.

While staying at Captain Horner's, Watson said, "Sundry of us made a sail boat excursion up the sound to the other boarding house on the same sound, twelve miles off, to the large house called 'Mansion of Health.' We found it well kept and supported by a goodly number of inmates. The house, a hundred and twenty feet long, stands about one-tenth of a mile from the surf. The original house once there was at one-half the distance and had numerous cedar and oak trees nigh it. The great September gale of 1821 swept over the whole island at this place and tore up or blew over those trees, so that none now remain nigh, although the stumps of many are still seen. The whole island is twenty miles long being from Tucker's to Barnegat Inlet. At its northern end are still many trees and high hills, wherein foxes burrow. As a riding vehicle to the surf and along the beach the ladies use an ox wagon, wherein they amuse themselves greatly in a rustic novel way. Gunners go there much in the season for wild geese and ducks. Inman has killed twenty-four geese in a day. Sheep, mules and horses are pastured and browsed on the northern end of the island, by himself and others. His house having formerly been the winter quarters for gunners, is fully cut with the names of his visitors, made on outside boards under the piazza."

The kindness of Mr. Nathaniel R. Ewan made the following data available to me. Richard Shreve, as a young man, was employed in the general store of his cousin, Joseph E. Hulme, of Wrightstown. This Richard Shreve later became the well-known Mount Holly mill owner, Richard Cox Shreve. He wrote a record of many of the early nineteenth century activities of Burlington County and in the late 1880's stated, "About the time I left the store at Wrightstown, I made my first trip to the seashore. Some well-to-do farmers had been in the habit of going to the upper end of Long Beach Island opposite Manahawkin. A man named Jimmy Crammer lived there and allowed the visitors to come in and do their cooking for a small compensation. The farmers would drive down through the pines and over the heavy sand roads. It was a day's journey. The farmers took their tents along and furnished their own provisions. They got tired of this and erected a large building which was called 'Mansion of Health,' and run by one Cushman of Philadelphia, at $3.00 per week per guest. Some thought this price so high they rebelled and he was compelled to close his house. The property was then bought by Hudson Buzby who ran it until it was destroyed by fire. So far as I know it was the first summer boarding house on the Jersey coast. The only way to reach the coast was by driving. The land was of little value."

Richard Coxe Shreve apparently visited the "Mansion of Health," and it is possible that a relative of his was connected with the boarding house for a time, since a Joshua Shreve is said to have succeeded Cushman as proprietor of the place and to have run it for several years.

J. H. Perrine had this to say about his family's connection with the place, "My uncle, George Bowker, my mother's brother, was proprietor of the 'Mansion of Health' at Great Swamp, now Surf City. He was there in 1875 when I was one year old for my mother had me there on June 12th, 1875, on my first birthday, and a gentleman placed a small gold dollar in my hand. I have been told that the place burned down within a year."

From these two statements we cannot tell whether the "Mansion of Health" burned down once or twice. It is quite certain that it burned down finally because an elderly lady informed me that her mother had told her that the "Mansion of Health" burned down in the 1870's and that within a few years shifting sands covered the ruins.

People in cities learned of these early seashore resorts through advertisements in newspapers and small handbills that were put up in public places. Some small notices were even handed around. Here is an advertisement that was distributed by Fulsom's Advertising Agency under date of June 30th, 1822.

SEA BATHING
Mount Holly and Manahawkin Stage

The Subscriber most respectfully informs the Public that he has commenced and intends running a Stage during the Summer Season for the accommodation of those disposed to Grouse Plains, Manahawkin or Tuckerton. The Stage will leave Manahawkin every Monday and Thursday morning and arrive at Griffith Owen's Tavern, Mount Holly, on the same evening, from which place Passengers will be carried to Burlington on the following morning in the regular line of Stages in time to meet the Steamboats for Philadelphia and Trenton.

Returning they will leave Burlington every Tuesday and Friday evening, lodge in Mount Holly and arrive in Manahawkin early the following evening, where ladies and gentlemen will be accommodated with genteel boarding and lodging at the moderate rate of three dollars per week, and conveyed at any time across the Bay to James Crammer's, Hazleton Cramer's and Stephen Inman's.

Fare through one dollar and twenty-cents.
                                    Seth Crane

A conveyance will be in readiness at Manahawkin for Tuckerton.

64   UNDER BARNEGAT'S BEAM

I have never been able to identify the Grouse Plains mentioned in this advertisement. Was it a settlement or a tavern? I have never been able to find it on any maps yet the name appears in at least one other advertisement of 1822. Griffith Owen's Tavern was one of the four famous taverns of Mount Holly. It was a small two-story building at the northwest corner of High and Water Streets and was established in 1749 by John Burr, Jr. The Washington House now occupies the site.

The three places mentioned across the Bay were all at Great Swamp. Stephen Inman's was the oldest. He would never take in more than four guests. James Crammer is the Jimmy Crammer referred to by Richard Cox Shreve. The following notation is found in the Surveyors Association of West Jersey Book, published in 1880 (page 299); "James, son of Josiah Crammer, 2nd., married Elizabeth, daughter of Jarvis Hazelton, of Manahawkin. Their children: Ann, Hazelton, Kesiah, Rachel, Elizabeth and Phoebe. For a long term of years James Crammer kept a boarding house at Great Swamp, opposite Manahawkin."

It is quite well established that Jimmy Crammer had two boarding houses at Great Swamp. And despite the spelling of a name in an advertisement, Hazelton "Cramer" was Jimmy Crammer's eldest son. Both father and son had boarding houses.

The following advertisement appeared in the "New Jersey Mirror and Burlington County Advertiser," for July 13, 1825:

SEA BATHING

The Great Swamp Long Beach Company informs the Public that they have now completed their elegant Establishment opposite Manahawkin, which now consists of a new Mansion, 90 by 28 feet, in addition to the house built a few years since by Mr. Crammer.

The House is finished and furnished in the best manner for the convenience and comfort of visitors, and the natural advantages which the situation possesses over any other on the Sea Coast are very great. In the first place, the distance in crossing the Bay is shorter and can be affected in either large or small boats, at any time with perfect safety. The distance from the House to the beach is but a few hundred yards and invalids will always be conveyed to and from the bathing in an easy and safe manner. There is a cool and delightful walk within a short distance of the House, through a beautiful grove of Cedars, to the Great Swamp. The managers assure the Public that no pains or expense will be spared to make the situation of those who may visit the Establishment, comfortable and agreeable.

Below this, in the same issue of the newspaper, was an advertisement illustrated by a stage coach with four prancing horses:

An elegant four horse Stage will leave Samuel H. Cooper's Ferry every Tuesday, Thursday and Saturday morning. Passengers will leave Arch Street Ferry at 5 o'clock a.m. and arrive at the Shore same evening in time to cross the Bay. Returning, leave every Monday, Wednesday and Friday morning, and arrive at Cooper's Ferry, same evening in time to cross over to Philadelphia in Steam Boat.

Fare through, $2.50—Stages commence running Tuesday, 12th inst.

White Robbins & Co.
July 5, 1825   Proprietors

Samuel H. Cooper's Ferry was at Pyne Point, now a part of North Camden. The Arch Street Ferry from Philadelphia landed here. This route to the seashore was a little longer than going via Mount Holly and the entire journey was by stage.

The Crammer house mentioned in the Great Swamp Long Beach advertisement was the last boarding house built there by Hazelton Crammer. A newspaper advertisement would seem to indicate that the "Mansion of Health" was owned by an incorporated company: "Notice: The Directors of the Great Swamp Long Beach Company request the stockholders to pay the last Installment of 15 dollars on each share to the Treasurer, Mr. Jennings by the 15th of July. Dated June 30, 1825."

The Ashley House

Whoever built the first boarding house on the north point of Long Beach built exceedingly well since it was used for a hundred years. The early records are not clear, but we do know that Jacob Herring purchased this building, named it the "Herring House," and then for a time did a thriving business. Jacob Herring, who was known as

"Jackey," and Garret G. Herring, who was Keeper of Barnegat Light from 1839 to 1841, were either brothers or father and son.

Captain John M. Brown, of Squan, a well-known wreck-master and salvager, acquired a run-down "Herring House" in the 1850's. The building was soon put in good repair by his four sons: Ashley, Lewis, Theodore and George. The captain's walk was added and the exterior of the building was painted white. The name was changed to "Ashley House" and it again became popular with gunners.

Ashley Brown was lost at sea in about 1860 and shortly thereafter the Brown family sold the place to Charles Martin, who was known up and down the beach as "Uncle Charlie." With the able assistance of his daughter Elizabeth, who was a famous cook, "Uncle Charlie" added to the prestige of the "Ashley House." In 1874, J. Warner Kinsey purchased the "Ashley House" from the Martins and renamed it the "Kinsey House." He operated it for about ten years after which the building was abandoned and finally torn down in 1887.

Captain Joseph Horner is said to have run Tucker's Boarding House for several years before he created a house of his own on Long Beach in 1815. This was some twenty years before the Tucker House burned down. Reuben Tucker retired to his farm in Tuckerton. This farm was part of Mordecai Andrews' original survey of 929 acres. Mordecai Andrews, Jr. inherited it and in turn gave it to his son Jacob Andrews who sold it to Reuben Tucker. The latter left it to his son Ebenezer Tucker, who sold it to James Sprague.

Captain Horner's new boarding house on the lower end of Long Beach prospered and was particularly popular with guests from Philadelphia, who bought it, added a few improvements and named it the "Philadelphia Company House."

The Long Beach House

In the 1840's, Lloyd Jones, of Tuckerton, where he managed the "Deacon House" for several years, built a sizeable boarding house on the south end of Long Beach near the "Philadelphia Company House." Then in 1851, Thomas Bond, a watch-case manufacturer of New York and often a guest at the Lloyd Jones House, purchased the property and changed the name to "The Long Beach House." This House stood near the Bay several miles below where Beach Haven now stands. Captain Bond's House was famous before there was a Beach Haven.

Thomas Bond lived here the year round and soon earned the title of "Captain." He was proprietor of a successful business for many years. The doings and customs at Captain Bond's "Long Beach House" have been, and will continue to be, written about for a long time. Failing health and the competition of the hotels and boarding houses in newly developed Beach Haven caused Captain Bond to lose his property in 1885 when creditors took it over. The creditors attempted to run the boarding house for a couple of years but had no success. The building was boarded up in 1888 and permitted to fall apart and decay. It was finally demolished in 1907.

Photographs of the "Long Beach House" show it to have been a large three-story "L" shaped building, with twenty windows on the west side which faced the Bay. There was a covered porch along this entire side. There was a three decked porch on the south side of the building, the upper porch being a popular vantage point from which to observe the sea. The short leg of the "L" had twelve windows on each floor.

CHAPTER X

BARNEGAT CITY AND ITS HOTELS

The 1880 edition of the "Seaside Directory of New Jersey" carried the advertisements of several hotels, boarding houses and developments on Long Beach. A full page announced the real estate development that gave Barnegat City its name.

B. F. Archer, Prest. W. Buzby, Vice Prest.
W. T. Bailey, Sec'y and Treas.
BARNEGAT CITY BEACH ASSOCIATION

Located on the north end of Long Beach, the first of the island beaches on the coast of New Jersey, which we meet coming from the north, stretching from Barnegat Inlet to Little Egg Harbor Inlet, being about twenty-one miles in length, having an average width of about one mile. This beach is virtually at sea, being separated from the mainland an average distance of about four miles. The broad bay and salt marshes lie between, and from this cause it has gained a reputation for salubriety and coolness in summer. The northern portion of the beach, where this company has located, has an altitude of several feet above any other portion. Its geographical position on the coast: air-line distance from New York, 60 miles; Philadelphia, 56 miles; in Longitude West 74° .06′ 12″, Latitude, North 39° 45′ 34″, forming the southern border of the well known "Barnegat Inlet," which opens on the largest body of water of its class which is considered wholly within the limits of the State; extends from Point Pleasant southward, to the place known as "Cedar Bonnet," opposite Manahawkin.

It abounds with Oysters of a fine quality, Fish of all varieties found on the coast, and Wild Fowl in their season. This Bay receives the waters of Metedeconk River, Kettle Creek, Toms River, Cedar Creek, Forked River, Oyster Creek, Gunning River, and several other small streams, and it may be safely stated that the portion of beach now in control of this Company . . .

HAS NO EQUAL in its Natural Attractions and Advantages.

It is the purpose of the Company to hold its old name "Barnegat" as it can only be mentioned suggestive of much interest, hence

BARNEGAT CITY BEACH ASSOCIATION.

The name is of Dutch origin, and can be safely traced back to Sir Edmund Ployden's pamphlet, describing New Albion (New Jersey) published in 1648, in which it is entitled "Sandy Barnegate." It has also been called "Baranda-gat."

There will be no hesitancy in bringing this valuable tract before the public, as the Company have already contracted for a Hotel with a capacity of 150 to 200 Guests, with 25 COTTAGES for the SUMMER of 1881.

Their interest covers about 600 acres, which will be developed with all practicability.

The hotel mentioned in this advertisement was the first of several erected in this locality. It was named the "Oceanic Hotel" and was built at Barnegat City. I am informed that it did not open until 1882 and that E. C. Boice was the proprietor for many years. Some contend that after the "Parry House" at Beach Haven burned down in 1883, its manager, Mark H. Buzby, moved up the beach to the "Oceanic."

The "Oceanic" finally closed in 1914 but for a number of years after its opening it was popular with Army and Navy officers and their families. The Hotel was originally erected on the beach but in a few years it was moved well back from the surf. It was washed by the sea in 1916 and a northeast gale in February, 1920, severely damaged it. The partially wrecked hotel building was purchased by Earl McAnney, who removed the furnishings and sold the building to Captain A. Richard Myers, who in turn salvaged most of the lumber, using it to build his pound houses on the Bay side. Thousands of bricks were salvaged which were cleaned by the young men of Barnegat City at the rate of fifty cents a hundred. The salvaged bricks were used for many purposes, most of them for the construction of the building at the Boulevard and Shore Road in Manahawkin.

The "Hesse," a little steamer, ran from Barnegat Pier to Barnegat City for several years. This was a Swiss lake steamer imported for this purpose but it did not last long since the salt water ruined the boilers. It was succeeded by another little steamer, the "Connecticut." The

Barnegat City steamer dock was at the upper end of Broadway, north of the "Sun Set Hotel"— both locations are now under water.

At one time Barnegat City had a horse-car line running from the steamer dock at the upper end of Broadway, down past the "Sun Set Hotel" and then over to the "Oceanic." Lewis Jones was the horse-car driver.

Harry Butterworth, of Mount Holly, was proprietor of the "Oceanic" for some years. Later he went to Harrisburg, Pennsylvania, where he and his brother, Mordecai Butterworth, kept the old "Bolton House."

There does not seem to be any truth in the oft-heard statement that the "Sun Set Hotel" in Barnegat City was originally known as the "Sans Souci." I have not been able to find any mention of a "Sans Souci Hotel" in any of the newspaper advertisements or directories. On the contrary, there is an advertisement of the "Sun Set Hotel" in Barnegat City in a Camden newspaper dated June 20th, 1884. This advertisement gave Ridgway and Braddock as the proprietors at the time. I am informed that Ridgway and Braddock built the "Sun Set Hotel" and that it was opened several years before the railroad reached Barnegat City. This might well make the opening date in 1884.

The "Sun Set Hotel" was owned and run by Captain A. Richard Myers when it burned down in June, 1932. It was located west of Broadway and north of Fourth Street, and its site has since been washed away by the swirling Bay waters. Prior to the proprietorship of Captain Myers it was owned and operated by John R. Barber, later of Spray Beach.

Barnegat City's third hotel, "The Social," was built in 1885 by William C. Kroeger and his wife. Mr. Kroeger was proprietor until his death in 1891. His widow successfully continued running the Hotel until 1915 when she sold it to Ernest Johnson and his wife. The Johnsons then sold it to Halvdan Ham and his wife who ran it as a restaurant and boarding house until 1953. It has been closed since then.

Barnegat City's newest hotel, the "Barnegat City Inn," was built by Mrs. Magna Hansen in 1927. This became a very popular place. Several years after Mrs. Hansen's death the "Inn" was sold to Ingman Benestad who ran it for a short time, and then sold it to Josephine Reider.

A railroad spur was built from Twelfth Street to the north end of the "Oceanic" after the Hotel had been moved well off the beach. After this, despite the fact that the main Barnegat City railroad station

BARNEGAT CITY AND ITS HOTELS

was at Twelfth Street, as were the engine house, water tank and coal bunker, most of the railroad business was transacted at the Fourth Street station alongside the "Oceanic."

The "Oceanic Hotel" erected a one story wooden pavilion on the beach at Fourth Street for its guests. A narrow boardwalk extended to Eighth Street where several bath houses were built. All this was washed away by the sea many years ago.

John W. Haddock, a retired Philadelphia business man, made his home on Fourth Street east of Central Avenue, and by 1910 his place had become famous. On either side of Haddock's front walk were miniatures of Barnegat Light about five feet tall. Scattered around his grounds were all sorts of articles salvaged from wrecked ships. His collection included figure heads, ship's wheels, ship's lamps and even a small pilot house. After his death the erosion of the sea made it necessary to move the house several times. The original site of the Haddock place is now at least three hundred feet out to sea under ten feet of water.

Mr. Haddock had an artesian well of which he was very proud. Although the site of the well is now submerged, Mr. F. Morse Archer, Jr., informs me that the well is still flowing and that he has been able to locate it several times by the temperature of the water.

CHAPTER XI

BEACH HAVEN IN THE 1880's

Embellished by the sketch of a two masted schooner with all sails set, the following advertisement appeared in the 1880 edition of the "Seaside Directory of New Jersey":

CLUB HOUSE
LONG BEACH, NEW JERSEY

All conveniences for	Competent Captains
GUNNING and	FISHING TACKLE
FISHING	AMMUNITION, ETC.

Capacity, from 30 to 40 Guests

TERMS: $2.00 per Day $10.00 per Week
    The place is unsurpassed for a good day's enjoyment.
Address: Jos. K. Ridgway, Proprietor

"Club House" was once quite popular with gunners and fishermen. But its written records and history, if they ever existed, were burned in the fire. Piecing together bits of available data along with the recollections of Alex. H. Inman, J. H. Perrine, Winfield Predmore, Clarence D. Gant and Captain Luther Carver, I have been able to obtain a fairly accurate history of this once well-known sportsman's club.

"Club House" was located about three-quarters of a mile north of Loveladies Life Saving Station. There were two main buildings. Some say they were erected in the 1830's and others in the 1840's. But it seems agreed that they were built by James James, who was known as "Double Jimmy."

It did not have the name "Club House" until the 1870's when a group of New York sportsmen purchased the property. Captain Charlie Cox of Barnegat, on the mainland, ran the "Club" for some years for this group. Then Captain Joe Ridgway took over the management. He was the advertiser.

George W. Van Note, who was proprietor of the "Carlton House" in

Tuckerton in the 1880's and 1890's, then became proprietor of the "Club." According to Alex Inman he was still there in 1909.

Davis Wright, a colored steward, ran the "Club House" for some years until the largest building burned down in about 1915. Shortly after the fire J. B. Kinsey bought the remaining building and stored baled sea weed in it until 1921. Then the "Club House" building was cut into two pieces and moved down the beach to High Point.

According to Captain Carver, who helped move the buildings down the beach, the oldest part of the "Club House" building, with its timbers carefully put together with miter joints and wooden pegs, was made into the apartment house at 81st Street across from the Harvey Cedars Post Office. The other half of the "Club House" building became "High Point Inn." It was a long narrow building on the east side of the Boulevard north of Kinsey's enlarged store. "High Point Inn" burned down in the 1930's.

Beach Haven had two hotels in the 1880's. The business card of the first read:

PARRY HOUSE
BEACH HAVEN
Ocean County, N. J.

An Elegant House surrounded by broad piazzas, overlooking the Atlantic Ocean on the east, and Tuckerton Bay on the west.

Has accommodations for 250 guests. Furnished with Spring Beds and Hair Mattresses. The table is furnished with the best the New York and Philadelphia markets afford. Alderney Milk and Fresh Vegetables furnished daily from the Proprietor's Farm. Polite and obliging servants, and everything to make the House home-like.

Darnell & Buzby,
Proprietors.

Unfortunately this Hotel burned down around 1885 while under the management of Mark H. Buzby and was never rebuilt. The "Parry House" was erected by and with the financial help of Charles T. Parry, of Philadelphia, and was named for him.

The second Beach Haven Hotel of the 1880's, the "Engleside," used a rather unusual form of advertising in that it gave a long list of references.

ENGLESIDE, BEACH HAVEN, NEW JERSEY
Rob't B. Engle, Proprietor

It is a new and handsome Hotel, with modern conveniences and appointments of a first-class house. It is beautifully located on an elevation, overlooking both Ocean and Bay, a fine view of which can be had from every bed-room in the House. The rooms are large and airy, and furnished with spring-beds and hair mattresses. It is the nearest house to the Beach in the place, and is one of the finest houses on the N. J. coast. Especial pains are always taken to have the table abundantly supplied with all the luxuries and delicacies of the place and season, and we challenge the world to produce better or purer drinking water than is furnished the guests of Engleside. References: Rev. Richard Newton, D. D., Church of the Epiphany, Philad'a; Rev. Charles D. Cooper, Church of the Holy Apostles, Philad'a; Jay Cooke, 114 S. Third St., Philad'a; Dell Noblitt, Jr., pres't of Corn Exchange Bank, Philad'a; Hon. Joseph Allison, 4207 Walnut St., Philad'a; Nelson F. Evans, 434 Walnut St., Philad'a; Frank H. Wyeth, 1412 Walnut St., Philad'a; Dr. Albert H. Smith, 1419 Walnut St., Philad'a; Hon. William B. Hanna, 2024 Race St., Philad'a; Bullock & Crenshaw, 528 Arch St., Philad'a; Rev. K. P. Ketchum, Plainfield, N. J.; Philip P. Dunn, Trenton, N. J.; Aldin C. Scovil, Camden, N. J.; William B. Sharp, Wilmington, Del.; Hon. Cortland Parker, Newark, N. J.; Alfred Henderson, Jersey City, N. J.; Dr. Bigler, Rochester, N. Y.; Henry Elwanger, Rochester, N. Y.; Josiah King, Editor of Pittsburgh Gazette, Pittsburgh, Pa.; Hon. Ormsby Phillips, Pittsburgh, Pa.; Mrs. General Howe, Pittsburgh, Pa.; Henry Holdship, Pittsburgh, Pa.

The "Seaside Directory of 1880" carried an advertisement and plan of "Stafford Beach," which was described as a magnificent property having a frontage of over four miles on the Atlantic Ocean and lower Barnegat Bay (Little Egg Harbor) and situated two miles below Beach Haven. Detailed maps and circulars were to be issued about May 1st (1880) at the office of The Stafford Beach Company, 113 South Fourth Street, Philadelphia. This development, it seems, never materialized.

CHAPTER XII

HARVEY CEDARS

There is a tradition that in about 1800 a white man named Daniel Harvey lived in a man-made cave on the knoll that marked the location of the former Harvey Cedars Hotel building. Some early American settlers lived in caves and while many began the immediate construction of log cabins, others improved their caves and continued to live in them for years. Such caves were occupied by settlers down the New Jersey coast among the sand dunes where Atlantic City now stands.

It is said that the present Harvey Cedars was first known as "Harvey's Whaling Station" and then as "Harvey's Hummock." According to several newspaper accounts the place was known as Harvey Cedars more than one hundred and twenty-five years ago.

It was called Harvey Cedars before Captain Samuel Perrine, Sr., remembered as Captain Sammy Perrine, erected the first Harvey Cedars Hotel on the knoll in the late 1830's. Some claim that Captain Sammy built his hotel around a little house that had been erected by one Sylvanus Cox in about 1813. Whether or not this is true will never be known since Captain Sammy's hotel burned down in about 1880 shortly after his death. He was proprietor of the hotel until the time of his death in 1876, although he died at his home in Barnegat, on the mainland, where his house still stands on Bay Street.

Captain Samuel Foreman Perrine, Jr.—the son of the elder Captain Sammy—was born in the Harvey Cedars Hotel on May 10, 1840. The Perrine family at times lived in the hotel. Captain Samuel Perrine, Jr. was the father of Joseph Howard Perrine, the designer and builder of sail boats, who was known as "J. H."

Captain Samuel Perrine, Jr. did not follow his father in the hotel business. He became first Keeper of the Barnegat Life Saving Station, being appointed November 22nd, 1872, and third Keeper of the Harvey Cedars Station, being appointed September 5th, 1879. His son, "J. H.," as a boy spent a portion of each year "on the beach," as mainlanders designated living on Long Beach.

The Schooner Yacht "Sans Souci"

Finally Captain Samuel Perrine, Jr., left the Life Boat Service to become full time skipper of the schooner yacht, "Sans Souci." As a matter of fact, for a while he was both Keeper of a Life Boat Station and skipper of the yacht. In those days Keepers of Life Boat Stations mustered their own crews for the nine months of the year during which they were on duty. They were off duty during the summer months.

J. H. Perrine was cook aboard the "Sans Souci" for several years and gave me an accurate description of the vessel. The "Sans Souci" was built at Barnegat on the mainland by Charles Sprague of Manahawkin. Costing twenty-five thousand dollars she was built for, and owned by, John Leisenring, of Mauch Chunk, Pennsylvania and Nathan Middleton of Philadelphia. She was used as a pleasure boat for their families and friends.

The "Sans Souci" was one hundred feet long, two-masted and schooner rigged. Her cabin was fifty-two feet long, twenty-six feet wide, with eight feet of headroom. The dining saloon was large and could accommodate twenty people. There was also a sizeable ladies' cabin with wash room and bath as well as six private staterooms, each with a marble washstand and built-in closet. The ladies' cabin contained a large sofa that could be converted into a double bed.

J. H. Perrine informed me that many times he provided for eighteen guests as well as a crew of ten. There was a large range and charcoal broiler in the galley. In the lower hold, under the cabin floor were two water tanks each of forty barrels capacity. There was also an ice chamber in the hold that held five tons of ice. Since the galley stove burned wood, a cord or so of fuel was stored in the hold.

The Captain's quarters were next to the galley and the crew's quarters were under the forward deck. The large, well stocked refrigerator was on the forward deck as was a large locker used for storing linens and blankets. An ample coat locker was filled with wool shirts, rubber coats and boots.

Captain Samuel Perrine, Jr. was skipper of the "Sans Souci" from the time she was launched in 1876 until she was abandoned in 1906. There was a black walnut table from the dining saloon of the "Sans Souci" in J. H. Perrine's home in Barnegat.

According to J. H. Perrine, the last person to use the "Sans Souci" was Mr. Leisenring's son-in-law, Mahlon S. Kammerer. He was a quiet man and would not permit any fishing on Sundays, spending those days in prayer and singing hymns with his family and friends. Mr. Kammerer was an early conservationist and no fish were caught unless they were needed for food aboard the ship.

Some say that Captain Sammy Perrine, Sr., first proprietor of Harvey Cedars Hotel, was Captain of the Volunteer Life Saving Crew at the northern end of Long Beach. Others say that Captain Predmore of Great Swamp was its leader. Opinions vary but both may be right. These volunteer crews functioned for more than twenty-five years before the establishment of the Federal Service and it is possible that there were two such crews between Great Swamp and the Inlet.

While it is certain that the first Harvey Cedars Hotel was built by Captain Samuel Perrine, Sr., in the 1830's and run by him and his family until his death, there is some uncertainty regarding the succeeding proprietors.

I quote from a statement made to me by J. H. Perrine, "After grand-father's death the Hotel was taken over by Captain Isaac Jennings, who ran it until his death, after which Dave White was in charge. Shortly after grand-father died the Hotel burned to the ground, but was immediately rebuilt the same as it was before and stood that way until Thompson changed it." This account differs from much that has been written about the Hotel and its proprietors but it is my belief that it is correct since it has been substantiated through two entirely different sources.

CHAPTER XIII

BUILDER OF BARNEGAT SNEAK BOXES — J. H. PERRINE

J. H. PERRINE, a Barnegatter and grand-son of Captain Sammy Perrine, Sr. began building boats at the turn of the century. His specialty was the Barnegat sneak box. During his fifty-five years in business more than thirty-six hundred boats left his yard. While everyone around the Bay knew these boats and many have sailed them, Perrine boats have been shipped to every State, to Europe, Africa, China and some of the Pacific islands. Many schools and yacht clubs used the fifteen foot sneak boxes to teach the rudiments of sailing.

The sneak box is peculiar to the Barnegat Bay region, its design having been worked out for the ever changing depth of water there. With its center board up it draws very little water and can go almost anywhere. Despite this the sneak box is very seaworthy in heavy weather.

J. H. Perrine patented his design of his boats and required parts could be ordered by number. The largest standard sneak boxes were twenty footers and the smallest twelve feet. They were either Marconi or Gaff rigged Sloop and Cat, with the majority having track on the spars. The largest boat ever built by J. H. Perrine in his yard was a forty-four foot yacht and the smallest a nine foot dinghy.

New Jersey cedar was used for the greater part of the construction. However, the center board, tiller and trim were either mahogany, oak or sassafrass. The spars were of spruce or fir.

The boat works were located in a frame building which was first a church, then enlarged to become the town school house. After a lapse of more than fifty years since it was used as a school blackboards were found on the inside walls.

The boat hulls were made on the first floor and the sails and rigging on the second. Triangular piles of cedar boards seasoning under proper outdoor conditions were found on the grass around the building. Cedar boards of the grade and width of those in these piles were hard to come by, but J. H. Perrine had a great knowledge of the South

BUILDER OF BARNEGAT SNEAK BOXES 79

Jersey cedar swamps and knew where the best timber might be found. He was assisted by his foster son, John Chadwick, with whom he lived.

Twenty-four decoy ducks stood on a shelf on the second floor of the boat works, blacks and blue bills. They were made by J. H. Perrine many years ago and the boat builder was very proud of them. Strangely enough these decoys had never been in the water.

My younger brother and I sailed our first Perrine sneak box in 1909 and since that time there has been at least one of these boats in our family almost continuously. My eldest son's twenty foot sneak box, built for him by J. H. Perrine, after his return from World War II, is one of his most cherished possessions.

Having shot ducks for more than thirty-five years west of Long Beach, it was natural for me to use a sneak box in both fair and dirty weather. I was on Goose Point when the winds ripped the nose out of the Shenandoah at Lakehurst, only some twenty miles away. The seas in the Bay that day were very wicked but I was safe in my sneak box. During a long period of years I have rowed, poled, sailed and pushed a twelve foot sneak box with an ice hook and the boat was dependable at all times.

Speaking of weather, J. H. Perrine informed me that he had seen the Bay frozen over many times and had walked, skated and ridden a bicycle on the ice. He recalled that his mother had told him she remembered when a young man named Sprague went sleighing on the Bay behind a two-horse team. The horses broke through the ice in the channel and were lost.

While his father, Captain Sammy Perrine, Jr. was Keeper of the Harvey Cedars Life Boat Station, J. H. Perrine and his companion, Joshua Milliard, who later became the loved and respected Dr. Milliard of Manahawkin, often walked down the beach to the great cedar tree known as the "Hawk" or "Owl" Tree. This tree was located about a mile below the Station House. The large tree was very much alive then and there were smaller trees around it. There were also large cedar trees south of the old Harvey Cedars Hotel near the bowling alley and dance hall and several on the west side of the Hotel.

As a youth I well remember the huge dead trunk of the "Hawk" or "Owl" Tree standing on the sand dunes on the beach well back from ordinary high water. Captain Ralph P. Smith informed me that he was surfman at the Harvey Cedars Station from 1915 to 1923 and that the great storm tide that broke through the lower end of Long Beach Island, making New Inlet in 1919, carried away the trunk of the "Hawk" Tree. Ralph also informed me that between the time he joined the Harvey Cedars crew and the great storm of 1919, the members of the crew transplanted the trunk of the dead "Hawk" Tree several times above high water before it was carried away.

Many will remember the scattering of sizeable cedar trees on the Surf City meadows and the dozen or so ancient cedar trees on the knoll south of Harvey Cedars Hotel. Many of these trees had trunks of considerable size, that would show them to be possibly four hundred years old. I recall but two still standing.

CHAPTER XIV

THE SECOND PROPRIETOR OF THE OLD HARVEY CEDARS HOTEL

Captain Isaac Jennings, of Manahawkin, was the second proprietor of the original Harvey Cedars Hotel. He was a salty old sea captain — crotchety and profane — who ran his Hotel as he had run his ships — giving orders as if he were on a quarter deck. He was a deep sea sailor who had many voyages, and took over the Hotel upon the death of Captain Sammy Perrine, Sr. and ran it with the help of his family until his own death in 1887.

After the first Hotel burned to the ground in about 1880, Captain Jennings rebuilt it "the same as it was before." But the Captain acquired partners in the rebuilding process. Some say they were Timothy P. Newell and Charles S. Ridgway, others claim they were Newell Ridgway and Granville Stokes. I believe they were the former two since they were then a well known Philadelphia importing firm with many interests in New Jersey. In any event, the partnership interests were sold and before 1900, the then well known William F. Thompson, the "Duke of Gloucester (New Jersey)" had acquired the whole property.

Although in poor health for many years, Captain Jennings died rather suddenly, a widower without children and leaving no will. Therefore his interest in the Hotel passed to his nieces and nephews and not to the brother and sisters of his wife who had worked with him in the Hotel for years.

David M. White, a step-brother of Captain Jennings' wife, went to the old Harvey Cedars Hotel in around 1876 and served in various capacities until he retired in 1906, having been connected with the Hotel for more than thirty years. First he assisted his sister and her husband in managing the Hotel, and after his sister's death managed it for the enfeebled Captain Jennings. After that he managed it for various interests.

Mrs. Emmor H. Lee has given me an account of her duties as a young girl when she lived at the old Harvey Cedars Hotel with her uncle and aunt, Captain and Mrs. Jennings. "Auntie brought me up, so that is why I was always there at the Hotel with her. My father, her favorite brother, died when I was a small baby. As a young girl I could not be of much use around the Hotel but I do remember that my daily duty was to see that every bed room had a new candle in the stick at all times and that the proper oil lamp was in each room with a freshly washed globe."

Mrs. Mary Bennett Jennings was a famous cook and under her supervision the dining room of the old Hotel became known for fine food. Her assistant was the affable colored cook—Amy—who took charge of the kitchen after the death of Mrs. Jennings. Amy maintained the high standards and became famous in her own right. Her snapper soup was on the menu every week-end and served all day on the Fourth of July.

Mrs. Jennie Ridgway, the assistant housekeeper, owned a pet crow whose favorite perch was the transom above the bar room door. Every so often a guest would discover that the crow was fond of sipping whisky from a glass. Too many sips always ended in the crow causing a great commotion and uttering unearthly cries which brought Mrs. Ridgway. After things had quieted down, Dave White would issue the solemn order, "Anyone seen giving the crow a sip of anything will not be served with further drinks from the bar."

The proprietors of the old Hotel ran it much like a farm. The gardens supplied early vegetables and certain staple ones during the entire season. There was a flock of chickens as well as a few cows, with a pig or two fattening. Mr. White took great pride in a flock of white ducks that lived in a shallow pond at the rear of the laundry. These ducks never swam in the creek which was less than a hundred feet away.

Mementoes of the Sea

Mr. White had another interesting hobby. He collected the name boards of ships wrecked on Long Beach and salvaged everything usable from these wrecks. All of the Hotel's firewood was cut up wreckage. This was hauled from the beach to the Hotel stable yard where there was always an interesting assortment of spars, rails, blocks and tackle of all sorts, awaiting the chopping block. The Hotel medicine chest had come from a wrecked vessel. In the front parlor were a child's cradle and chairs that had been salvaged.

Mr. White used the name boards of the wrecked ships in an original manner. These were either plain or scrolled panels on which were carved the names of the ships. Such boards were usually found on either side of the ship's bow. The name of a ship and its home port were usually painted across the stern.

Every building in the Hotel yard had one or more of these boards nailed to it, often over the door. The storage house had two—over one door was the name board of the "James Jones," wrecked in 1883, and over the other door the more elaborately carved board of the "Albertine Meyer," which was piled up on the beach early in 1884. An oversized dog house, seldom occupied by a dog but usually used by the hens, was open at both ends and sported two name boards, these were of the "Dixie" and "Magnolia"—two barges that had been wrecked at the same time in 1893. The well ventilated barn that had been standing for many years had the prosaic name "Hapwood."

The open-faced chicken house, seldom used by the fowls who preferred the dog house and nearby cedar trees, was named for a lady—"Altavela"—and on the inner wall was the name board of the "Deceiver." Both vessels had gone to pieces in 1884. The name on the ice house came from the Scotch vessel "Aberdeen."

Each stall in the stable had a name board, "Simla," "Guadalupe," and "Dexter," high sounding names for horses that had to endure insects in the summer. The pig sty, situated farthest from the Hotel, was held together by three pieces of timber bearing the names "Henry Finch," "Lida Babcock" and "Hayes," the latter two ships were wrecked in the 1880's.

None of these buildings remain and the name boards disappeared with them. Most of these name boards came from vessels wrecked on the northern end of Long Beach Island between 1880 and 1900. I have a recollection of some of the better specimens of name boards having been stored above the rafters in the wagon shed. These beautifully carved panels and scrolls of finely grained woods would be museum pieces today.

A finely carved and painted figure-head stood upon a pile of stones just beyond the west porch of the old Hotel. It was the figure of a woman, about eight feet tall, dressed in the period of the Civil War. No one knew from what ship she came and the guests called her "Hannah." This figure-head disappeared in 1903. Since it was then in excellent condition it is hoped that it has been preserved.

CHAPTER XV

THE END OF THE FIRST HARVEY CEDARS HOTEL

The old Harvey Cedars Hotel finally closed in the spring of 1903, but before work was begun on alterations and renovations, a public sale was held of the furnishings and equipment. Dave White was proprietor of the renovated hotel when it reopened on October 15th, 1903.

The old Harvey Cedars Hotel was not torn down as is so often implied. It was merely jacked up and a cellar built beneath it to house the well pump, lighting and heating plants. The present Hotel was then erected around the old building, the old hotel being the west portion of the present building. The center hall-way and the east, or ocean side of the building are new as are the dining room and kitchen. Firman Crammer of Manahawkin was the contractor.

The oldest employee of the Hotel in point of years was the handyman, Riley Rogers. Among his many other duties he was in charge of the slatted snapper pen. This pen was so located that the overflow from the Hotel well drained through it. When Amy, the cook, required a snapper, which was at least once a week, Riley would reach into the pen, pick a twenty pound specimen up by the tail, and carry the hissing, snapping reptile to the chopping block near the stable. Placing the snapper on the block, he would permit it to get a good hold on a heavy stick with its mouth. Then he would stretch the neck and off would come the head with a single blow.

Riley was also in charge of the ice house where all perishables were kept under salt hay. Former employees of the Hotel have told me that salt ice was cut in the creek and put in the ice house, while fresh water ice was cut on the ice pond or brought over from Manahawkin Lake.

Mr. Francis Fenimore, an old resident of Harvey Cedars who moved to Hollywood, Florida, recalled the fresh ice pond. It was built above ground between Captain Lukens' "Atlantic House" and his grand-father's big beach cottage. The pond was man made, its sides built up of turf. These sides were about two feet above ground level and the fresh water came from the Lukens' well, being pumped to the pond by the windmill. Mr. Fenimore informed me that the old Harvey

THE END OF THE FIRST HARVEY CEDARS HOTEL 85

Cedars Hotel ice house was still in existence. It had been moved northward from close to the hotel kitchen door to the vicinity of the Horse Bridge where it was converted into a cottage.

The sea turf used to build up the sides of the fresh ice pond was cut from the meadow just north of Jason Fenimore's cottage on the east bank of the creek. This cottage still stands. The removal of the turf made a body of water perhaps fifteen feet wide and forty feet long. This was called the canal and since it was several feet deep it made a fine harbor for small house-boats.

One of these house-boats, berthed in the canal forty or fifty years ago, was the "Olive.' Richard F. Holeman, of Mount Holly, knew the "Olive" well and described her for me. She was owned jointly by Dr. Joshua Milliard of Manahawkin, George W. French of Mount Holly, and Mr. Holeman's father.

The "Olive" was about twenty-eight feet long and nine feet beam. There were two bunks on each side of the cabin as well as three windows. The wheel was starboard of the forward hatch inside the cabin. There was a single cylinder four cycle gas engine. She had double floors so that the cabin was always dry. By using the hand rail it was possible to go from the forward to the after deck without going through the cabin.

Returning to Riley Rogers and his varied duties—he was also master of the stables. There were always a couple of horses and sometimes a mule. The two wagons were both springless. Riley drove one of these wagons to the Harvey Cedars railroad station to meet the trains from Camden.

The only boardwalk Harvey Cedars ever had was about twelve feet wide and almost a hundred feet long. It was really a wooden bridge going from the southeast corner of the Hotel to the Harvey Cedars railroad station, crossing the creek and the little island. This boardwalk was in existence until about twenty-five years ago when the ice took part of it and it was never repaired.

There were only two roads in old Harvey Cedars. One was a very narrow gravel path which began at the rear of the big Francis Fenimore house on the beach and went south, parallel to the beach, to Crammer's cottage near the Life Saving Station. The other was the Hotel's private road and the only one really used until the Boulevard was built. This road extended from the north end of the Hotel buildings to the railroad station. It was "U" shaped and a little over a half mile long, following the west bank of the creek to the narrowest point where a wooden bridge was built out of some wreckage from the beach. This was known as the "Horse Bridge" because Riley could always find a loose plank which he could flip up so that his grazing horses could not leave the island. A concrete bridge crosses the creek at this point today.

The oyster house on the west bank of the creek and the oyster float anchored in the center were also in Riley's domain. There was an old flat-bottomed boat tied to a stake and whenever a call came from the kitchen for oysters or clams Riley rowed out to the float. He never counted the oysters or clams he opened, simply filling the kettle or jar given him.

Floral Sneak Boxes

Riley Rogers also had an eye for beauty. When a sneak box was hopelessly beyond repair it was pulled up on the knoll on the west side of the Hotel and he took charge. He put several inches of sand in the bottom of the boat and then a layer of small sharks, skates and the like, to which he added a shovelful of broken oyster and clam shells. Atop this he placed a few inches of soil brought over from the mainland. Into this he stuck a few geranium shoots and some nasturtium and petunia seeds. In a few weeks the Hotel had a colorful display of flowers.

Several party boat captains always lived at the Hotel. I can well recall Captains Frank Martin and Thomas Ridgway, and later Captain Les Malcolm of Barnegat and Captain Ike Horner of Parkertown. Boat rates for a family fishing party were five dollars a day with the captain furnishing the bait.

The party fishing boats were all sail boats, center board sloops carrying as part of their equipment one or two peeled cedar pushing poles along the deck. These were called "setting poles." When the wind fell, many a fishing party was poled to its home dock, possibly a few hours late. Up until 1910 most of the motor boats carried these cedar poles.

A sneak box was always towed behind the sloop. The Bay flats were then covered with long waving eel grass, the natural breeding place for crabs and shrimp. The captain would anchor his sloop at the location he intended to fish and then go off in the sneak box for bait.

CHAPTER XVI

A FAMILY DEDICATED TO A HOTEL

Martha Moore might almost be regarded as the "mother" of the Harvey Cedars Hotel. Four of her children were connected with the management of the Hotel through the years from 1876 to 1909. She herself was born in Manahawkin in 1805 and married twice.

Her first husband was Samuel Bennett and four children were born of this marriage—three daughters and a son. The eldest was Mary Ann. Martha Moore's second husband was John White, of Mount Holly, whom she married in 1836. Eight children were born of this union— Anna Eliza, Alanson, Miriam, Hannah, Martha, John Moore, Joanna S., Joseph Henry and David M., the latter being born in 1850. John White, the father, was killed by a runaway horse when David M. was quite young.

Mary Ann Bennett, the eldest daughter, taught school in Manahawkin for several years before she married Captain Isaac Jennings, the second proprietor of Harvey Cedars Hotel. Captain and Mrs. Jennings had no children of their own so they surrounded themselves with members of Mrs. Jennings' family. They raised her niece, Liby, the daughter of Alanson, who died shortly after his only child was born. Liby John White became Mrs. Emmor H. Lee of Moorestown. David M. White moved to the Hotel as a young man to be followed by his sisters Hannah and Joanna.

Captain Jennings became quite enfeebled after his wife's death and David M. White, who was known up and down Long Beach Island and the mainland as "Dave" White, assumed management of the old Harvey Cedars Hotel for his brother-in-law until the latter died in 1887. During Mrs. Jennings' lifetime, her sister, Hannah Martha White, assisted her as housekeeper of the Hotel. After Mrs. Jennings' death Hannah remained as housekeeper and after the Captain's death she stayed on with her brother Dave. She was housekeeper until about 1900 when she retired.

Before her retirement, Hannah Martha White prevailed upon her younger sister Joanna S. White to come to the Hotel. Joanna became housekeeper upon her sister's retirement. She also held this position in the enlarged Harvey Cedars Hotel and after David M. White retired she was proprietor of the Hotel in 1906 and 1907. After this she went to one of the larger hotels in Cape May.

David M. White married Mary Hazelton of Manahawkin. Being a strict Baptist she refused to live at the Hotel, objecting to the bar. The David White homestead on the Manahawkin-Tuckertown Road still stands. Until a few years ago it could be easily identified by two huge South Sea fluted clam shells, one on either side of the front steps. These had previously been in the parlor of the Harvey Cedars Hotel. The shells were stolen from the door step a few years ago.

A Distinguished Guest

Mrs. Emmor H. Lee, my mother—Mrs. William J. Kraft—and Mr. Josiah E. Willitts of Haddonfield, have called my attention to the fact that William Spencer, of Chester County, Pennsylvania, successful light opera composer, was a regular guest at the old Harvey Cedars Hotel for several seasons.

His "The Little Tycoon" opened at the Temple Theatre, Philadelphia, on January 4th, 1886. It was an instant success. The Temple Theatre burned down but the play moved to the Arch Street Theatre and then to the Academy of Music. After this the play enjoyed success on the road for some six years.

Willard Spencer's next success was "Princess Bonnie" which opened at the Chestnut Street Theatre on March 26th, 1894. It remained for a run of 1040 performances. Miss Leanora Mayo, who became Mrs. James Elverson, Jr., was the star and Ethel Jackson, later of "Merry Widow" fame, played in "Princess Bonnie" for the entire run. Spencer's third success was "Miss Bob White" which opened in April of 1901, starring Ethel Jackson and featuring Raymond Hitchcock, who had been in the chorus of "The Little Tycoon."

It was Spencer's habit to come down to the old Harvey Cedars Hotel while he was working on both "Princess Bonnie" and "Miss Bob White." He would go out in the Bay alone in a cat boat, sometimes taking his luncheon but more often just a jug of cold water.

He would find a quiet place and drop anchor and there compose his music and write his lyrics. Spencer composed the music and wrote the lyrics for his plays. Often he would be gone for the entire day but was never far from the Hotel, possibly a mile or two at the most.

CHAPTER XVII

HARVEY CEDARS LANDMARKS OF THE PAST

The "Atlantic House," a large boarding house opposite the Harvey Cedars Railroad Station, was erected in about 1877 by William and John Smith, brothers, of Brown's Mills, New Jersey. The Smiths operated the general store at Brown's Mills for years and were succeeded by Squire Warner Hargrove, after they went to Pemberton where they operated the grist mill. Captain Howard Lukens operated the "Atlantic House" for many years. The building was destroyed by fire in November of 1911.

The Club house of the often mentioned "Seven Cedars Club," "Penrose Club," and "Harvey Cedars Outing Club" was best known locally as the "Bungalow." It was originally built as a summer place by William H. Sayen, of Philadelphia, president of a railroad.

The building was quite large with the kitchen across the north end and the living room across the south end. Between the two were about a dozen bed rooms with baths. A porch, fourteen feet wide, covered the east, south and west sides. Hughey Bolton, Sr., of Manahawkin, was caretaker of the "Bungalow" for some years prior to 1925. The "Bungalow" burned down in 1930.

Several years ago, while at the home of Mr. Oscar Twitchell, in Haddonfield, I was surprised when Mr. Burleigh B. Draper, dean of Camden bankers, said to me, "I can tell you when the Sayen bungalow at Harvey Cedars was erected. The year was 1885 and the contractor was my father, Thomas W. Draper, of Philadelphia. I will never forget it. We sailed across the Bay from Manahawkin and I lived in the bunk house with the carpenters for several days."

Mr. Sayen did considerable entertaining after the railroad bridge crossed the Bay. There were sometimes so many guests that the "Bungalow" could not accommodate them all. A siding was laid at the Harvey Cedars stop near the engine house of the Manahawkin, Long Beach Transportation Company and Pullman sleeping cars were placed on this siding furnishing sleeping accommodations for the male guests while the ladies slept at the "Bungalow" where all meals were served. Mr. Sayen was president of the Manahawkin, Long Beach Railroad as well as of the larger railroad and Francis Fenimore was treasurer of the local Company.

The largest house in Harvey Cedars was that of Francis Fenimore of St. David's, Pennsylvania. It was on the beach beyond the "Atlantic House" and was built in about 1892. Mr. Fenimore was a gentleman farmer and decided to have a fine lawn around his house. The top soil was brought from the mainland in freight cars but after replacing the lawn several times after severe winter storms the idea was abandoned.

About 1909 the encroaching sea made it necessary to move this fine big house from its original position to one some several hundred feet back from the high water line. The hurricane of September 14th, 1944, completed the wrecking of this house.

The Jason Fenimore cottage on the east bank of the creek just south of the railroad station was built about 1894. Captain Leslie Malcolm, of Barnegat, a former deep sea captain, looked after the Fenimore property. Captain "Les" as he was affectionately known lived in a little house-boat moored in the canal. He was a great fisherman.

The bathing pavilions of both Harvey Cedars and Surf City apparently were built from the same plans. They were almost identical and are said to have been erected by the developers of the places in the late 1880's. The Harvey Cedars pavilion was moved back from the high water mark at the same time the Fenimore house was moved. However, the hurricane of September, 1944, demolished this pavilion as well as the one at Surf City.

Beginning around 1904, Harvey Cedars had its own school for a time. It was known as District School No. 3 and was housed in a building that had been erected in 1892 as Francis Fenimore's cow barn. This building was later moved down to Jason Fenimore's boat house on the creek bank when he became Clerk of the Borough of Harvey Cedars. In about 1906 the school-room was moved to the southeast living room of the big Francis Fenimore house. While this room had a large fireplace, still a big tin stove was used to heat it. Miss Lottie Sprague of Manahawkin was the teacher. The cow barn—school—borough hall later carried a sign which I still remember—"Bachelors' Hall"—which proclaimed the use to which the building was put from 1908 onward.

The railroad stations on Long Beach Island were all built within a year or two after the trains came to the Island. The Harvey Cedars

Station with its wooden platform and freight floor was erected in 1890; and the engine house, water tank and wind mill were erected in 1894.

There were two wind mills quite close together. The taller of the two was that of the railroad, while the shorter one was known as Captain Lukens' wind mill. The latter really belonged to Francis Fenimore but served two places. When the tank of the "Atlantic House" was full, a valve was turned, and then water was pumped into the lead lined tank in the third floor tower room of the Fenimore house.

The first club on Long Beach was probably the Peahala Club, north of Beach Haven. It is said that "Peahala" is pure Indian meaning "duck." This club was established in 1882 by Jerseymen mostly from Burlington County. They acquired the holdings, land and house of Captain Thomas Jones who had run a well known boarding house for fishermen and gunners.

Shortly before 1900 a new club house was built just off the beach. The old building was left standing to take care of over-flow guests. The new club house stood for some forty years when it was torn down and the land sold to real estate developers.

For years the "Peahala Club" was one of New Jersey's most famous duck shooting organizations, most of the birds being shot around Daniel's Island. According to Mr. Nathaniel R. Ewan some of the old members were; Hezekiah B. Smith of Smithville, Isaac Harrison of Chesterfield, John Hutchinson of Bordentown, Evan Buzby and Daniel Woolman of Rancocas, William B. Wills and Edward Stokes— co-owners of the "Mt. Holly Herald," and Mahlon Green—proprietor of the then well known "Green's Hotel" of Philadelphia.

CHAPTER XVIII

HARVEY CEDARS FIFTY YEARS AGO

Harvey Cedars in 1909—fifty years ago—had very few buildings. The northern boundary of old Harvey Cedars began at Buffalo Point on the Bay shore and extended across the Horse Bridge to the beach. The southern boundary extended from the ocean to the Bay just south of the graveled yard of the Harvey Cedars Life Saving Station. The Harvey Cedars of today is many times that size.

Going back to 1909—we will begin at the north line and proceed southward. The building nearest the north line was the enlarged Harvey Cedars Hotel which was surrounded by four or five outbuildings. Then, to the south of the Hotel, and situated on its own island reached by a gravel path and a narrow bridge, was the "Penrose Club" better known as the "Bungalow."

Going eastward, across the boardwalk from the Hotel, was the railroad station. Across the railroad tracks were Captain Howard Lukens' "Atlantic House" with its cook house and wind mill; the railroad round house, wind mill and water tank. Jason Fenimore's cottage and boat house were on the east creek bank.

Continuing down the path—past the Lukens' property to the ocean, there was, on the right, the huge storm battered sumer home of Francis Fenimore. Across the path from the Francis Fenimore house, and a little to the north of it, was the Harvey Cedars Bathing Pavilion. This bathing pavilion had some forty bath houses on the first floor. The second floor was a huge covered porch with the stairs to the cupola going up the center. The cupola was ten or twelve feet square and a good forty feet in height.

The Cramer cottage was about half a mile down the beach. Then, toward the Bay, was the only two family house then in Harvey Cedars. It was known as the Ridgway cottage. Then came the Conrad cottage with the original Life Saving Station, which had been converted into a house by Captain Howard Lukens, across from it. Then came the Life Saving Station with several small buildings just outside its graveled yard. These were used as workshops by the crew and to house gunners in the duck season.

That was all there was to Harvey Cedars in 1909. There were no buildings for several miles to the south to the Surf City line except a very airy seaweed house used for storing baled seaweed which at that time was used for stuffing furniture. A cluster of buildings called High Point was a good half-mile to the north of the Buffalo Point-Horse Bridge line. High Point had its own post office and railroad station.

Of all the buildings mentioned only four are standing today; the Harvey Cedars Hotel, the Jason Fenimore cottage on the east bank of the creek, the Life Saving Station and the Ridgway cottage, which, although battered by a hurricane, was moved down the Bay shore and rebuilt. The Life Saving Station, which was built in 1901, when the first Station was no longer large enough to accommodate the crew and equipment, is now occupied by the "Long Beach Island Fishing Club."

I have been unable to find a description of the Harvey Cedars Hotel when it was run by Captain Sammy Perrine but have seen two paintings purporting to show the Hotel at that time. Comparing these paintings with photographs taken prior to 1900 along with J. H. Perrine's statement that after the fire the Hotel was rebuilt "the same as before," I am convinced that a description of the second Hotel would also cover the first.

The old Harvey Cedars Hotel was a long frame building of two stories and an attic. It was built close to the ground there being but one step to the porch. For the most part the building was one room wide, the covered porch on the west side acting as a hall for the first floor bed rooms.

The parlor was at the south end of the building, its only door opening onto the screened south porch. This room was seldom used although the door was never locked. A little stove always had a fire in it and a couple of great vases were filled with dry cat-tails. Adjoining the parlor were five or six bed rooms. There were no bath rooms. Each bed room had a wash stand with a large china bowl and pitcher. Light was supplied by candles and small kerosene lamps.

The little office was next to the bed rooms on the first floor. This office had a small counter on which was the well worn, leather bound hotel register. Unfortunately this book was destroyed some thirty-five years ago. In addition to the names of guests it contained a store of information about great storms, records of catches of fish and bags of game and other data.

Now the Hotel widened out and became two rooms wide. The room facing the Bay was the bar room with its fireplace and gun racks. The other was the dining room with three long tables. The dining room table nearest the kitchen door was the first, or proprietor's, table. The proprietor sat at this table with the fishing boat captains and several male guests. The kitchen was beyond the dining room.

The bed rooms on the second floor were not as long as those on the first since a narrow hall way ran along the west wall of the building. The attic was one large room with a double line of single beds. Here the fishing boat captains slept.

I can never recall the Harvey Cedars Hotel, old or new, without a substantial dock extending out into Barnegat Bay. The dock was about three hundred feet long, but only a third of it extended into the Bay, most of it being board-walk over the meadow. It had a small rectangular bulk-head at the end made from solid timbers from some wrecked ship. This bulk-head was filled with oyster and clam shells. Although long neglected this dock weathered all storms until the 1920's. The dance hall was a one story building with a peaked roof located southwest of the Hotel beyond the potato cellar. Later it was moved north of the Hotel and became a chicken house.

CHAPTER XIX

RAILROADS AND ROADS
TO
LONG BEACH

The railroad bridge crossing the Bay from Manahawkin Meadow to the island of Long Beach was erected in 1885-1886 and was almost totally destroyed by a northwest storm in mid-November 1935.

Before the railroad bridge was built visitors to Long Beach took trains from Philadelphia and New York to certain mainland rail-heads and were then ferried across the Bay in small steamers. These steamers ran from Toms River, Forked River, Barnegat Pier and Edge Cove. There were horse cars running on light rails from the steamer docks to the hotels at both Barnegat City and Beach Haven.

The railroad bridge from Manahawkin Meadow to Barnegat City was a timber trestle of three hundred and ninety spans having a total length of 4,859 feet with one "draw" just east of "Martin's." The last railroad station and stop on the mainland meadow was "Milliard's," almost at the Bay edge. "Martin's" was the first station across the Bay and was so-called because Humphrey Martin and his wife kept a little boarding house on an island which is now the "Bonnett Clubhouse." This station was actually on the bridge at the west edge of the channel where the hand-manipulated draw was placed.

The first station and stop on Long Beach was "Barnegat City Junction." This was several hundred feet east of "Martin's." All trains stopped at "Barnegat City Junction." There was a "Y" at the Junction. At first, when the railroad bridge was completed, the Pennsylvania Railroad trains from Camden ran up to Barnegat City (now Barnegat Light) since the tracks were first laid to that end of the island. Then the trains went down the Island toward Beach Haven as far as the tracks were laid. The first train arrived in Barnegat City early in July of 1886. The tracks to Beach Haven were not completed until some weeks later.

The Certificate of Organization of the "Philadelphia and Beach Haven Railroad Company," was dated December 29th, 1893 and was filed in the Office of the Secretary of State of New Jersey, January 13, 1894. This represented a re-organization of the "Long Beach Island Railroad Company," and a portion of the latter Company's railroad was acquired by the "Barnegat Railroad Company."

The Philadelphia and Beach Haven line extended from Manahawkin to Beach Haven, a distance of 12.12 miles, connecting with the "Barnegat Railroad" at "Barnegat City Junction." This whole system had been constructed in 1886 by the "Long Beach Island Railroad Company," and was acquired by the Pennsylvania Railroad in December, 1893, at a foreclosure sale.

After the regular train service stopped going to the northern portion of Long Beach — from Barnegat City Junction to Barnegat City — the "Manahawkin, Long Beach Transportation Company" began operation in the early 1890's. This line extended from the Junction to Barnegat City.

The rolling stock of the "Manahawkin, Long Beach Company" was interesting. First there was the "Dummy," built at the Baldwin Locomotive works in Philadelphia for the 1893 summer season. This was a one car "train." The engine was placed in front part together with an upright boiler and coal bin. There were gears to drive the solid front wheels while the four smaller rear wheels were truck mounted.

Jason L. Fenimore, Sr., who was to become engineer of the "Dummy," made the trip from the locomotive works in Philadelphia to Barnegat City as a passenger when it was delivered. On this trip the "Dummy" traveled on its own steam from Camden to Long Beach early in 1893.

In addition to the "Dummy" there was a small sized three car train known as the "Yellow Jacket," because the cars were painted a bright yellow and the little engine which had no pilot wheels, was painted black. Car No. 1 was a combination baggage-passenger car and unless it was the only car on the "train" served as a smoker. Cars No. 2 and 3 were diminutive passenger cars having but twelve windows and double seats on a side. The entire train was standard gauge as was the "Dummy."

The "Yellow Jacket" cars seem to have been consumed in a forest fire on the mainland near Barnegat but the little locomotive survived and was used for many years. The No. 2 engine of this railroad was a little larger than that of the "Yellow Jacket" and smoked very badly, hence it was called the "Tar Pot."

The stations and stops between Barnegat City Junction and Barnegat City were: Surf City, with its station; then "Hay Station" which was a "flexible" stop depending upon who was cutting salt hay or gathering seaweed and where. After this came Kinsey's Seaweed House which was a shelter of sorts for storing baled seaweed, and Conrad's, the platform at the Harvey Cedars Life Saving Station. Now came Harvey Cedars with its wooden platform, freight platform and small station building.

After this came High Point with its small station; then Loveladies, a platform at the Loveladies Island Life Saving Station; Club House, a gravel platform, and Twelfth Street, Barnegat City. This was the largest station with an apartment above it. Finally came Fourth Street, with a gravel platform alongside the "Oceanic Hotel" and the busiest station of all.

Mrs. Minnie D. Kelly informed me that the "Pennsylvania Railroad Roll of Honor" of November 30th, 1918, disclosed that George Heisler was appointed track foreman, July 26th, 1886, at Barnegat City on the Barnegat Railroad, which was abandoned for a time. The Company still had a contract to carry the United States Mail between Barnegat City and Barnegat Junction. Heisler was detailed to carry out this contract and carry the mail by hand-car. This was quite a task but when the wind was right he rigged a sneak box sail on his hand-car to help him on his way.

The railroad to Long Beach was in operation until November 16th, 1935, when operation was discontinued because of destruction of the bridge across the Bay. Traffic had been decreasing for many years so that the railroad could not be operated on a profitable basis and the reconstruction of the bridge was not warranted. The railroad was abandoned in 1936, upon the approval of the Interstate Commerce Commission under date of March 16th, 1936. The "Philadelphia and Beach Haven Railroad Company" was dissolved June 24th, 1937. The entire capital stock of the Company amounting to $200,000 was owned by the Pennsylvania Railroad at the time of dissolution.

The first and only vehicle bridge across the Bay from the mainland to Long Beach Island was built in 1913-1914 by a private corporation. Since mid-November 1935, when the railroad bridge was carried away, this causeway has been the sole means of entering or leaving Long Beach other than by boat. Another bridge is being built south of the present one.

The vehicle bridge was built about 800 feet south of the railroad bridge and cost about one hundred thousand dollars. It is a wooden bridge almost a mile in length and spans the bay water from Manahawkin meadows on the mainland to Ship Bottom on the island. This was a toll bridge until it was purchased by Ocean County. It was officially opened June 20th, 1914. Storms have battered it despite the fact that it is at the narrowest part of the Bay.

CHAPTER XX

A FASCINATING ENDEAVOR — TRACING OLD NAMES

Tracing old place names mentioned in letters and identifying their present locations is a fascinating and rewarding endeavor. It is equally interesting to identify individuals mentioned in old documents since spellings of the same name often differ. These place names and people often played an important, but now largely forgotten part in the War for Independence. All this was particularly true in the Little Egg Harbour area with its seamen and privateers.

Forks of Little Egg Harbour

The following two letters are of particular interest. The first appeared in the "Year Book of the Atlantic County Historical Society," October, 1952, while the second letter is privately owned.

President of the Council of Safety of New Jersey.

Forks of Little Egg Harbour, June 12, 1777

Sir: We this morning received information from Cap't Bradley of the Foxborough, that on the 10th inst. about six o'clock in the evening, a brig appeared off Little Egg Harbour Inlet, and made a signal for a pilot. Joseph Sowey with his brother and two boys went off to conduct it into port and were taken and carried off. Immediately on taking them on board the brig proceeded to the mouth of Great Egg Harbour Inlet, where she again threw out a signal for a pilot, on which Mr. Golder went off in his boat and on approaching near enough, finding she was a vessel of force, he immediately put about and pushed for the shore, the enemy's boat pursuing with only two men showing themselves. On coming within a hundred yards, a number of men showed themselves and fired on Golder and crew, who with difficulty gained the shore, but was obliged to quit their boat, which fell into the hands of the enemy.

99

As Sowey is one of our best pilots, we doubt not that he will be made use of by the enemy to bring in their tenders, and pilot them up the bay and river, which may be productive of most fatal consequences, the inhabitants being in a most helpless condition and having a great number of cattle and other property that must immediately fall in the hands of the pirates unless some spirited steps were immediately taken to prevent it. We have presumed to take from Cap't Shaler, eight or ten pieces of cannon belonging to a Sloop of his lately cast away on the coast, which we have this day, ordered to Foxborough, under his direction, with orders to immediately throw up a battery to defend the Inlet, and to annoy the enemy as much as possible, should they attempt to enter. There are now at Foxborough a guard of about twenty men, and Col. Clark will immediately order down as many more, to assist in doing the necessary work, Shot can be procured here (Batsto). We doubt not that the Council will think it expedient to lose no time giving the necessary directions for ending what they think ought to be done on this alarming occasion.

We are, with great respect, your most ob't and h'l ser'ts
John Cox
Elijah Clark

The second letter covering the same subject was sent to Charles Pettit of Burlington, a member of the Council of Safety and first Secretary of State of New Jersey under the first State Constitution.

Batsto, Friday Eve., June 13, 1777

My dear Friend: As the bearer waits I have only time to inform you that a few days ago a brig appeared off Little Egg Harbour Inlet & Decoyed Joseph Lowey & two other of his boys and that yesterday afternoon a Brig of 18, a Sloop of 12, and a Schooner of 8 and a pilot boat of 6 guns were piloted over the bar and are now at Foxburrough and in possession of a Brig in which I am concerned just ready for sea & a very fine vessel belonging to Wilmington, and I take it for granted will continue there as there are some vessels expected hourly from sea of which I dare say Lowey has informed them. I yesterday wrote a letter to the Council of Safety advising them of Lowey's being taken off & that I expected he would pilot in Tenders & sent it to Haddonfield but the messenger is returned & informs me that the Governor and Council were all dispersed and he brought back the letter. I think it highly necessary they should know the situation we are in. I shall go down to Chestnut Neck tomorrow with a number of Men in order to erect a small Fortification of 8 or ten guns to prevent them if possible from penetrating the Country. I am, in haste   Esteened and Most Hb. Svt.

John Cox

As for the place names mentioned in these letters, "Foxborough" is the Fox Burrow of today. The meadow hasn't changed since Revolutionary times and is still unimproved and unspoiled. It is now owned by a friend of my family who takes great pride in its preservation. Only a year or so ago my eldest son had his best day of duck shooting on this meadow.

The exact location of "Forks of Little Egg Harbour" has long been controversial. The first letter suggests that "shot can be obtained there (Batsto)" and I am inclined to agree with the few who are of the opinion that "Forks of Little Egg Harbour" and "Batsto" were one and the same busy place.

The Joseph Sowey and Joseph Lowey mentioned in the two letters are one and the same person, being attempts at an English spelling of the name of an early settler — Yose or Joseph Sooy. He was a Dutchman who settled at Lower Bank, on the Mullica River, in Washington Township. Although he had been captured by the British, called "pirates" in the letter, and forced to pilot ships across the bar, Sooy and his family were patriots.

John Cox, then owner of Batsto Furnace, was active in the affairs of New Jersey and in March, 1778, was appointed Assistant Quarter Master General of the Continental Army.

Colonel Elijah Clark was an officer in the State Militia and a member of a pioneer Mullica Hill family. He was a very religious man and in 1756 built what became known as "Clark's Log Meeting House" at Pleasant Mills. The Methodist Church erected there in 1808 occupies the site of this Meeting House.

"Clark's Landing," one of the earliest villages on the south bank of the Mullica River, was founded by the Colonel's ancestors. It was about fifteen miles from the Bay and at one time was a very busy shipping center for salt hay, cord wood, charcoal and iron products from Gloucester Furnace which was near Lower Bank. Even after the Revolution, and as late as 1818, "Clark's Landing" had forty dwellings, some two hundred inhabitants, an active church and a well established trading post.

Today nothing remains but two marble grave markers identifying the graves of Thomas and Ruth Clark who died in about 1750. Some years ago James Beauchamp Clark, better known as Senator Champ Clark, had these grave markers reset in concrete blocks, thus permanently marking the site of Clark's Landing Burial Ground, from which, even at that time, most of the graves had been washed away by the encroaching river tides.

The "Forks of Little Egg Harbour" became a very busy place during the Revolution. Privateers took a heavy toll of British shipping and were using the Inlet at will. Advertisements for the sale of prize ships frequently appeared in Philadelphia newspapers since most of New Jersey's legal advertising was placed in Philadelphia papers where it would be seen by more people. The following advertisements are taken from "The Pennsylvania Journal" and "The Pennsylvania Packet," both of which had many subscribers in New Jersey.

State of New Jersey, May 13, 1780
TO BE SOLD

at Public Vendue, on Monday, 29th inst. at the house of Mr. Richard Westcott; at the Forks of Little Egg Harbour River, the Sloop "Swallow", burden about 70 tons, with four three-pounders and four swivels, together with all her tackle, apparel, furniture; also pork, beef, bread, powder, ball &c. Captured by Captain Nathan Brown and others.

By order of his Honour the Judge of Admiralty
Z. A. Rossell, Marshal

N. B.: Cash is expected at time of Sale.

State of New Jersey, May 16, 1780.
To be SOLD by PUBLIC VENDUE

On Monday, the 29th of this instant, at the house of Mr. Richard Westcott, at the Forks of Little Egg Harbour River, the Prize Brig "BLACK SNAKE," the Schooner "MORNING STAR" with their tackle, apparel &c. Captured by Captain William Marinner.

Zachariah Rossell, Marshal

A FASCINATING ENDEAVOR — TRACING OLD NAMES   103

To be SOLD by PUBLIC VENDUE

On Tuesday, the eighteenth of this instant, at the house of Colonel Richard Westcott, at the Forks of Little Egg Harbour, The SCHOONER "HETSEY," burden about thirty tons, with her cargo of turpentine consisting of fifty barrels.

Also the SLOOP "REVENGE" mounting two carriage guns and four swivels, agreeable to inventories, to be seen at place of sale. They are both very fast sailers.

Zachariah Rossell, Marshal

At the time of the above mentioned VENDUE, will be SOLD, the PRIVATE SCHOONER "LITTLE MOLLY," formerly called "Yankey Witch" mounting two two-pounders and six swivels, with all her material, agreeable to inventory, to be seen at time of sale.

Joseph Ball

This Joseph Ball was apparently the manager of Batsto Furnace. Colonel Richard Wescott, or Westcoat as the name is sometimes spelled, served several years with the Continental Army and was badly wounded at the Battle of Trenton. After the War he moved to May's Landing where he died at the age of one hundred and two years.

The ships offered for sale at the Forks of Little Egg Harbour were almost all prize ships captured by privateers and little of the cargo offered was of local origin. Practically all of the ships sold were armed. The continued and successful depredations against British shipping by these privateers became so annoying to the enemy that the following year a sizeable expedition was sent from New York to attempt to stop it.

John Bacon — Outlaw

On October 23rd, 1782, a small British ship bound for New York, with a general cargo, grounded on the bar on the south side of Barnegat Inlet. How long it was there before it was sighted by Captain Andrew Steelman, an ardent Patriot of Cape May commanding the armed vessel "Alligator," is not known. Captain Steelman seized the grounded ship.

Meanwhile Captain John Bacon, a notorious refugee and his Tory raiders sailed across Barnegat Bay from the mainland with a full knowledge of the grounded ship and its location.

Captain Steelman, with his crew of perhaps twelve men and with the assistance of some local men, began salvaging the cargo. Among the local men was Reuben Soper of Soper's Landing on the mainland near Barnegat. The cargo contained a number of chests of Hyson tea, a much favored and extremely scarce article in the Colonies at that time.

The salvage crew brought their boats safely through the surf several times with boxes and bales from the grounded ship. At the end of the day the salvaged cargo was stacked on the beach and some of the crew camped beside it.

During the night Bacon and his men attacked the salvage crew and killed or wounded the entire group of nine. Captain Steelman and Reuben Soper were killed. John Bacon and the known members of his band were declared outlaws. A price of fifty pounds was placed on his head and half that amount on the heads of each of his followers, including one Ichabod Johnson.

Knowing every trail and road in the deep tangled forests of the mainland, Bacon and his men evaded capture. On December 27th, 1782, a party of Burlington County Militia, six horse and twenty infantry, searched the sea shore area without success. Returning, these militiamen stopped at the inn at Cedar Bridge.

Suddenly Bacon's outlaws appeared on the bridge. Captain Benjamin Shreve, in command of the Militia, succeeded in forcing the bridge, but finding himself alone had to dash back through Bacon's outlaws. The Militia lost two men. William Cook, Jr. of Cook's Mills was killed and Robert Reckless of Recklesstown (now Chesterfield) was mortally wounded. The outlaw Ichabod Johnson was killed.

The hunt for Bacon and his outlaws continued. On April 3rd, 1783, another detachment of New Jersey Militia was more fortunate. Led by Captain John Stewart, of Arneytown, a small party of soldiers surprised John Bacon while he was calling on a young woman.

Some say this was at Will Rose's Tavern between Tuckerton and West Creek — others say that it was at Red Tavern on the old New Gretna-Tuckerton stage road. In any event John Bacon was trapped. But he did not surrender. Waiting his time he attempted to run for the woods but was shot down by the soldiers. Thus ended the career of New Jersey's most notorious outlaw.

Batsto and Bog Iron

The bog iron furnaces in the New Jersey pine woods played a major role in the American struggle for independence. Their employees were exempt from military service so that a supply of iron might be assured the Colonists. The "ore" used by these furnaces was commonly known as "bog" or "swamp" iron and was a variety of Limonite.

Batsto and bog iron are synonymous to Jerseymen. A furnace was established here in the 1760's and according to tradition the name is an Indian word meaning "Bathing Place." Colonel John Cox owned Batsto Furnace during the Revolution, but the advertisements of the Furnace indicate that even during the war the production was not confined to military materials. An advertisement from "The Pennsylvania Journal" under date of May 8th, 1776, gives a list of the products.

MANUFACTURED AT BATSTO FURNACE

In West-New-Jersey, and to be SOLD at either the works, or by the subscriber in Philadelphia — A great variety of iron pots; kettles; Dutch ovens; and oval fish kettles, either with or without covers; skillets of different sizes, being much lighter, neater and superior in quality to any imported from Great Britain — Pot ash and other large kettles, from 30 to 125 gallons; sugar mill gudgeons, neatly polished and rounded at the ends; grating bars of different lengths; grist-mill rounds; weights of all sizes from 7 to 54 lbs.; Fullers plates; open and close stoves of different sizes; rag-wheel irons for saw-mills; pestles and mortars; sash weight and forge hammers of the best quality. Also Batsto Pig Iron, as usually the quality of which is too well known to need recommendation.

John Cox

It is surprising that salt pans have been omitted from the long list of items mentioned in this advertisement. Batsto Furnace salt pans were used in many of the salt works that dotted the salt water bays along the coast. Some of these were still in operation in the 1820's.

Charles Read of Philadelphia assisted in establishing several other bog iron furnaces in the south New Jersey woods near the Batsto Furnace. They were Etna or Aetna Furnace, near present Medford Lakes; Taunton Furnace, shown on some old maps as Read's Mill;

and Atsion Furnace. Read and his associates owned and controlled large holdings of woodland. Wood and water were the two main requisites for running a bog iron furnace. The wood of several hundred acres was needed to supply the charcoal necessary to run one of these furnaces for a year. There were continuous advertisements in the newspapers for wood-cutters, two shillings six pence having been the standard price for cutting one cord.

Charles Read moved to Burlington and became prominent in the affairs of New Jersey, rising to Acting Chief Justice in 1764. Alice Thibou Read, his wife, a native of Antigua, West Indies, is buried in old St. Mary's Burial Ground in Burlington. Charles Read died in obscurity in North Carolina.

That the early furnace owners had difficulty with labor is shown by the following advertisement from the "New York Gazette and Weekly Mercury." This advertisement also refers to the location of Batsto.

June 24, 1776

TEN DOLLARS REWARD

Run-away from Batsto Furnace last night two Spanish Servant Men, one of them named Francis Barrara, about thirty years of age, about six feet two inches High, black Hair, brown Eyes, and thin Visage, takes a Quantity of Snuff, his foreteeth remarkably wide, and has a down Look. Had on, and took with him, one blue Cloth short Coat, one light brown Duffles under Jacket, one new pair Oznabrigs Trowsers, Oznabrigs Shirt, a Pair of Half Worn Shoes, and half-worn Hat with a broad Brim. The other named Francis Rordigo, but goes by the name of Joseph, about five feet five or six inches High, yellow Complexion, black Hair and brown Eyes. Had on and took with him, one blue Cloth short Coat, light brown Duffles under Jacket, one Pair dove-coloured Plush Breeches, one pair new Oznabrigs Trowsers, Oznabrigs Shirt, one Pair half-worn Shoes, and an old Hat. Whoever takes up with the above RUNAWAYS, and secures them in any Goal, so that their Master, Mr. John Cox of Burlington, may have them again, or delivers them at Batsto Furnace, shall receive the above Reward and reasonable Charges.

Joseph Ball

N. B. This is the second time Barrara has runaway.

Batsto Furnace is at the Forks of Little Egg Harbour

A FASCINATING ENDEAVOR – TRACING OLD NAMES 107

Joseph Ball, who signed this advertisement, and his wife Sarah, gave the building and ground to the Batsto-Pleasant Mills M. E. Church in 1808. Several cast iron grave markers, with names and dates cast in them, may be found in the burying ground surrounding the church.

Fire backs made of New Jersey bog iron are quite rare and are collectors' items. Those made at Batsto are particularly scarce. I have seen three and have heard of one more. All are museum pieces.

Norwood H. Andrews and I visited the exceptionally fine Colonial residence of Mrs. Henry Ridgely, on the "Green," in Dover, Delaware, on "Dover Day," 1952. This outstanding American home was erected in 1728 by Thomas Parks and acquired by Charles Ridgely in 1764, and has been in the possession of his descendants ever since.

By chance we noticed a magnificent Batsto fireback of singular design and in good condition at the back of one of the fireplaces on the first floor of this house. It was of a design new to me and had been in the house for about one hundred and fifty years. Mrs. Ridgely kindly gave me the history of this fireback.

Miss Mary Middleton of "Barriton Fields," near Salem, New Jersey, first married Captain Benjamin Vining. After Captain Vining's death, his widow, Mary Middleton Vining, married a widower, Nicholas Ridgely, of Annapolis, Maryland. Their families, both had children by their prior marriages, moved to Dover, Delaware, in the late 1730's. John Vining, a son of Captain Vining and Mary Middleton Vining, became Chief Justice of Delaware. The Chief Justice first married Rachael Ridgely, the daughter of his step-father. She died while a very young woman. He then married Phoebe Wynkoof. Mary Vining was born of this second marriage.

General Anthony Wayne (1745-1796) was affianced to Mary Vining. His gift to her was a Lowestoft tea set which is today in Mrs. Ridgely's home in Dover. Unfortunately General Wayne died in 1796 just before the wedding date. Chief Justice Vining is believed to have died in "Barriton Fields" while on a visit there with his wife and daughter. This fine Batsto fireback has remained in the Ridgely ancestral home in Dover since it was brought there from New Jersey prior to 1800.

CHAPTER XXI

BARNEGAT COOKERY

There seems no more fitting way to close a book than leaving the readers with something they can partake of themselves. You may now go into your kitchen and prepare dishes that will bring the lore and lure of old Barnegat into your home.

The salt air of Long Beach whetted the appetites of all — summer visitors seeking rest and relaxation as well as duck hunters and fishermen seeking sport. Through the years this challenge has been met by those who prepared the clams, oysters, fish and other hearty foods in a most delectable manner.

It has been my pleasure to have enjoyed the cookery of Barnegat and from the many recipes — all good — I append the following which I share with you.

Clam Fritters

Mrs. Jason Fenimore made clam fritters that excelled all others. While confined in my home by illness in December of 1952, Ted Barber of Barnegat Light visited me. We talked of many things and memories of Long Beach Island and then we talked of Mrs. Fenimore's clam fritters. Fortunately her oldest son, Francis Fenimore, living in Florida, had his mother's famous recipe and forwarded it to me.

No quantities are given in Mrs. Fenimore's recipe since several things must be considered such as the number and size of the clams used, individual appetites and number of guests.

However, *two large clams per person* will be ample unless you are cooking for duck hunters — in which case keep cooking until they stop eating.

Drain the clams from the juice (which may be used for other purposes). Put clams in chopping bowl with a small piece of onion or a drop or two of onion juice — always remembering that a little onion goes a long way.

Chop clams well (DO NOT GRIND): add a dash of salt, pepper, cayenne, Worcestershire Sauce (this may be omitted if desired), a pinch of ground nutmeg, or cinnamon, or ginger: at least one well beaten egg (depending on quantity): and a little milk or clam juice. Stir well.

This mixture when well stirred should be wet but not watery. Then sift in flour and mix with a spoon. Use just enough flour to hold the mixture together nicely.

To about a quart of this mixture placed in a fairly large bowl, add one or two tablespoonsful of baking powder dissolved in a little milk. It will expand.

Place a large frying pan on the stove with just enough bacon fat or lard to thinly cover the bottom. Replenish fat as used up.

When the pan and fat are properly heated, drop large tablespoonsful of this clam mixture into the hot fat. As soon as holes form on the top of the frying fritter, turn it. In a short time — about one minute — the fritter will be ready to serve.

Clam fritters are like hot cakes, they should be served on hot plates as soon as they come off the fire. They should be nicely browned — even burnt around the edges. Too much grease will make them soggy, but too little will burn them.

Deviled Clams

This is a favorite family recipe. Our children and friends are very fond of these deviled clams as made by my wife.

Drain a dozen large clams, keeping the juice. Run the clams through a grinder. Simmer one slice of minced onion in three tablespoonsful of butter in large frying pan until tender. But do *not* brown onion. Then stir in one level tablespoonful of flour, add one cup of milk. Stir until well blended and smooth.

Put clam juice in small saucepan and let come to a boil; skim off froth. Add one cup of boiled, strained clam juice to the mixture in the frying pan; add minced clams; two cups of soft bread crumbs (no crusts): one teaspoon Worcestershire Sauce; salt and pepper to taste. Beat one egg slightly and stir into cooking clam mixture. Stir until thickened. Put in clam shell halves. Sprinkle tops with bread crumbs and dot with butter. Bake until brown on top.

Clam Chowder

Nearly everyone along the coast has a recipe for this great dish. Here is an old favorite.

Put the iron stew pot on the stove. Into this goes a half pound of diced salt pork. Try this out but do not burn. Remove the grease. To the browned salt pork add whatever vegetables you wish. These generally are potatoes, celery, carrots, and a slice of onion, all cut small, but *never grind* the vegetables. Add one half of the strained boiled clam juice, a cup of water, a pinch of salt (remember clams are salty), pepper, a bay leaf or two, half a teaspoon of sugar. When the vegetables are cooked tender measure them in cups. Add a cup full of chopped clams floating in a little clam juice for each cup full of vegetables. Add the balance of the clam juice. Cook for five minutes and serve piping hot. *Be sure to have enough clams* and do not overcook them since they toughen.

Put a piece of butter on top of each bowl of chowder and serve piping hot.

Clam Broth

This delicious broth can be served at any time during the day or night and making it is quite simple. It is enjoyed by all in our family and the recipe came from my wife's relatives in Baltimore.

Scrub the shells of a half dozen or more chowder clams and put them, just as they are, in a covered kettle with just enough water to cover them. Let come to a boil. The clams will open up as the water boils. After boiling for ten minutes take the clams out and throw them away. Skim any foam from the broth.

The broth is now ready to serve as it is — real hot. Some prefer it with a little hot milk or cream added. Whichever way served, first put a piece of butter in the cup and pour the hot broth over it. Season to taste, but most prefer it without the addition of pepper. Salt is seldom required.

Fried Oysters

Along the Delaware River they are known as Fortesque Fries but down Manahawkin-Tuckerton way they are plain fried oysters. These oysters are not encased in that thick mass of egg, corn meal and cracker crumbs that puff a little oyster to king size.

These oysters are fried in THIN batter, flour, oyster juice, or part oyster juice and part milk or butter-milk, and a pinch of salt. The batter must be thin. Pat oysters on dry towel or napkin, dip in batter, and fry in small frying pan in a bit of butter. When browned to your favorite color turn. The best results are obtained when the oysters are fried a half-dozen at a time.

Escalloped Oysters

A tasty dish that takes a bit of doing but well worth it. Seldom met with.

Drain at least thirty oysters and keep juice. Strain the juice through cheese cloth.

In a baking dish arrange a layer of say ten oysters. Cover lightly with a cup and one-half of buttered bread crumbs. Season with one-quarter teaspoonful of salt, one thirty-second teaspoon of cayenne and a dash of nutmeg. Moisten this with one-eighth cup of the strained oyster juice.

Repeat this procedure for layers two and three, adding three or so dabs of butter on top layer.

Bake in hot oven for a good twenty minutes.

The above is my preference but some cooks add cream, green peppers, celery and any number of things.

To make buttered bread crumbs: melt three tablespoonsful of butter in a small pan, stir in three cups of stale bread crumbs (no crusts). Season with salt and white pepper, stir lightly over heat with fork until crumbs are evenly covered with butter.

Deviled Crabs

This recipe has many friends among our acquaintances who generally prefer it out of a baking dish rather than in individual crab shells.

Make a very thick white sauce out of three tablespoons of butter, four tablespoons of flour and one-half cup of milk. Season to taste with salt and pepper, nutmeg and chopped parsely. Mix well.

Add at least a pound of nice crab meat. Stir well. Reheat and put the mixture in a baking dish. Sprinkle top with bread crumbs and dabs of butter. Put in medium oven until nicely browned on top.

Should any be left over, use it the next day. Put a snitch of butter in a small frying pan and place the crab mixture in the pan. This makes a delightful semi-crab cake.

Croaker Bouillon

I first tasted this aboard Captain Jens Jensen's dragger "Gertrude J," and have never forgotten its delicious flavor. Serve piping hot with a big round cracker.

Scale and clean a large croaker. Cut off the tail, cut out the fins and gills, BUT leave the head on. Put whole fish in stew pot with enough water to cover. Add two whole onions, bay leaf, salt and pepper.

Boil about fifteen minutes. Lift fish out of the broth carefully for other uses. Fish will make fine fish-cakes or fish salad.

Strain bouillon into sauce pan. Check seasoning and serve hot.

Fish Chowder

Using a large bass, Mrs. Helen Schoening, wife of Big Ed. Schoening, the troller, made fish chowder that was delicious. This should be made in sufficient quantity to insure "seconds" and a bit for another day.

Cut ¾ pounds of salt pork into small cubes. Brown nicely in frying pan. When sufficiently browned put in a stew pot with four quarts of water, and one cup each of diced carrots and celery; ¾ cup diced onions. Boil for twenty-five minutes. Add two cups of diced potatoes. Boil ten minutes.

Tie a three or four pound sea bass in a cloth. The bass should be cut into 1½ inch pieces, include the head with gills cut out. Simmer in stew pot slowly for a good ten minutes. Take the fish out and let it cool. Pick the fish meat from the skin and bones and put back into the chowder kettle. Stir well and serve hot. Season to taste.

Fish Soup

Mrs. John Larsen, wife of Captain John Larsen, who skippered the dragger "Mary Ann" for years and then the head fishing boat, "Miss Barnegat Light," was noted for this delectable soup.

Boil four or five pounds of nicely cleaned fish (including heads with gills cut out) in sufficient water to cover. Boil for one-half hour. Remove fish from broth. The boiled fish may be used for other purposes or picked from the bones and added to the soup just before serving.

Make a "cream sauce" using the fish broth in place of milk. In another pan cook the desired quantities of cut up onions and carrots. When cooked add to the "cream" soup. Season to taste and sprinkle top with chopped parsley. The more fish the better the soup.

Baked Bonita

The secret of successfully baking bonita, which is a fine fish, is in having the fish very clean and wiped dry before cooking it.

Stuff the fish with your favorite bread filling and score both sides before putting it in baking pan. Smear a little lard on bottom side of fish and lay bacon in the scores along the top of the fish.

Bake in moderate oven until flesh cleaves from the bones. Time for baking will vary with size of the fish but trying with a fork after the first twenty-five minutes will keep one abreast of the situation.

If the fish is not done enough it will taste "fishy," if done too long it will be dry. Go lightly on salt and pepper.

Boiled Beef

Boiled beef dinners were a welcome change along the coast before the days of electric refrigerators. They were delicious.

Put the following in a sizeable iron pot on the stove: a four or five pound piece of lean beef, a couple of quarts of water, a bay leaf, salt, pepper and a pinch of thyme. Place lid on pot and boil beef for an hour.

Add vegetables such as quartered potatoes, cup up carrots, diced celery, small onions, cut string beans and green lima beans.

If fresh vegetables are scarce use a handful of dried lima beans or a can of corn. Canned tomatoes are never used, except as a separate vegetable to be used as "gravy" for plain boiled potatoes, or as a side dish with browned croutons.

Boil the beef with the vegetables for about an hour: thicken the juice with browned flour or mashed potatoes. Cut the boiled beef into slices at least one-half inch thick. Have freshly ground horse-radish handy or have horse-radish sauce for the beef and serve the vegetables on the side.

Beefsteak Pan Gravy

Hughie always pan broiled our steaks in a large frying pan. When the steaks were done to his satisfaction and placed on a large platter for carving; he poured just a little of the fat out of the frying pan. Then he put the rest back on the stove and used a cup and a half of boiled black coffee, instead of boiling water, to make the pan gravy. Try this.

Irish Stew

This was always a favorite at our shooting shanty.

Into an iron stew kettle, provided with a tight lid, went about three pounds of lean lamb cut into bite-size pieces. This was covered with salted water and brought to a boil. Then it was allowed to simmer for about three hours and any grease was skimmed off.

Then were added 12 whole small onions, the same number of potatoes cut in quarters, six carrots cut in sizeable pieces and plenty of cut-up string beans.

This was simmered for another hour, then thickened with either browned flour or mashed potatoes. Then were added two tablespoonsful of chopped parsley, a bit of basil, majoram, savory, some cut up celery and a bay leaf. Dumplings made into walnut size were finally added. If too much of the liquid steamed away this was compensated for by replenishing the stew with boiling water or chicken broth.

Coffee

The coffee served at our shooting shanty was made in a large old fashioned agate coffee pot.

A heaping soupspoonful of coarsely ground coffee for each cup wanted was put into the pot. Then one was added "for the pot." Water was measured in the size cups used, the same number of cups of water as there were soupspoonsful of coffee. The shells of several eggs were added, or if some forty cups of coffee were being made an egg was broken into the pot and the shell dropped in.

The coffee was then brought to a boil — care being taken that it did not boil over — since that seemed to affect the flavor. The coffee was permitted to boil for three good minutes then a cup of cold water was added to "settle" it. It was let stand about three minutes before pouring. Some cooks added a pinch of salt to the pot just before serving.

Egg Harbor Harrier

There appear to be many fancy recipes for this now, but here is an old and tried one still used by many mainland families.

Put a large iron stew pot on the stove over a low fire. Cover the bottom of the pot with thin strips of salt pork or bacon. Keep turning these until brown on both sides and about half-done. Add a layer of sliced onions; and then a layer of potatoes sliced about one-half inch thick. A little cut-up celery or carrots, parsnips or turnips may be added if desired.

If your harrier is to be made with eels, now add a layer of eels cut in two inch pieces.

Repeat everything except the salt pork or bacon. There should be at least two layers of everything. Cover with water and let simmer: add salt and pepper, a bay leaf, some thyme and paprika. Replace lid and let simmer until vegetables are done.

Add thickening for the gravy, adding hot water to keep the ingredients covered. Stir a bit to get a nicely thickened gravy and when it begins to bubble put slices of bread on the gravy. Let steam give the bread some flavor. Then with a large ladle put a piece of this bread on each plate and cover with a generous helping of the harrier.

Some people make this with clams. If you do, leave out the eels, and proceed as above. Cut plenty of clams in quarters and bring them to a boil in their own juice. Do not cook clams too long as they may toughen. Add the cut up clams to the pot of thickened vegetables. Do not add clam juice. Stir well and serve.

Venison Stew

This recipe has been chosen by me from many venison stews I have eaten in various parts of America. The recipe generally meets with the approval of the ladies. We must remember that good venison stew takes time to prepare.

Cut the venison into bite-size pieces after removing all fat, bone, gristle and sinew. After venison has been prepared place in a large frying pan over a low flame. Put in a tablespoonful of Crisco or oleo, or mix them. Replenish this as it is used up.

Add to the layer of the cut-up venison a cup of cut-up celery leaves. A tablespoonful of cut-up green peppers may also be added if desired. Dust with a bit of flour. Place lid on pan. Stir occasionally until venison cubes are browned.

Place at least a four quart iron stew pot (furnished with a tight lid) over another burner. Turn the flame down a bit. Place a piece of butter and one medium sized chopped onion in this pot. When this is tender add two cups of water, a bouillon cube and a bay leaf and let simmer.

When the first pan of venison is properly browned, put it into stew pot and repeat browning until all venison is used up. The stew pot is meanwhile simmering all the time.

Now half cook the vegetables desired in a small quantity of water in a sauce pan. These vegetables may be quartered potatoes, carrots cut in quarter inch discs, green lima beans, tomatoes, string beans and peas. Only delicately flavored vegetables should be used. When these vegetables are half cooked, place them water and all, into the stew kettle which has been simmering under a tight lid.

Always simmer venison stew to retain flavor. Season to taste with salt and freshly ground pepper. Add a dash or two of Worcestershire Sauce.

Now back to the pan the venison was browned in. Heat it again and add a piece of butter and enough flour to thicken the stew gravy when it has been browned. Stir the flour in the frying pan so that it browns but does not burn. Then add this to the simmering stew.

Increase the flame under the stew kettle so that all is properly mixed. Stir constantly for possibly ten minutes. Let simmer another half hour with occasional stirring so that it does not burn. Add a pinch of cinnamon and several pinches of marjoram. Be sure the lid is on tight while stew is simmering. Now move to back of stove and serve with a ladle.

AUTHORITIES CONSULTED

Annual Report of Operations of the United States Life-Saving Service, etc., for Fiscal year Ending June 30, 1882.
Washington, Government Printing Office 1883.

Books and Maps, Geographical Society of Philadelphia

Newspapers, maps, relics, etc. Museum and Library, Burlington County Historical Society

Newspapers, maps etc., Museum and Library Camden County Historical Society

General Services Administration, National Archives and Records, Washington, D. C.

United States Coast Guard
Washington, D. C.

Salter, Edwin, "A History of Monmouth and Ocean Counties" Bayonne, E. Gardner & Sons, 1890

Gordon, Thomas F., "The History of New Jersey from its Discovery by Europeans." Trenton, Daniel Fenton, 1834

Watson, John F., "Annals of Philadelphia and Pennsylvania in the Olden Times." Published by the author, 1850 (2 Volumes)

Gummere, Amelia Mott, "Friends in Burlington"
Philadelphia, Collins, 1884

Published by Order of the Society, "Constitution, By-laws etc., of the Surveyors' Association of West New Jersey"
Camden, S. Chew, 1880

Alexander George Findlay, F.R.G.S.
"Description and List of the Lighthouses of the World 1872-3" 13th. Edition, London, Published for Richard Holmes Laurie, 53, Fleet Street, E.C. 1873

INDEX

Abbot, Dr. Charles, 20
Absecon, 22, 24
Anchor (or Anchoring) Island, 4
Andrews, Edward, 6
"Ashley House," 65
"Atlantic House," 84, 89

Bacon, John (outlaw), 103
Ball, Joseph, 103, 107
Barnegat (name), 21
Barnegat Bay, 22
Barnegat City, 68
"Barnegat City Beach Association," 68
"Barnegat City Inn," 70
Barnegat City Junction, 95
Barnegat Inlet, 9
Barnegat Life Boat Station, 31
Barnegat Lighthouse, 41
Barnegat Pier, 95
"Barnegat Railroad Co.," 96
Barnegat Sneak Boxes, 78
Bartlett's Coaling Dock, 95
Batsto, 100, 101, 105
Beach Haven, 2, 72
Beef (Boiled), 1, 113
Beefsteak Pan Gravy, 114
Boarding Houses (early), 61
Bog Iron, 105
Bond, Captain Thomas, 27
Bonita (Baked), 113
Bouillon (Croaker), 112
Bridge (railroad), 95: (vehicle), 97
Brotherton, 15
"Bungalow," 89
"Burning Hole," 21

Cabot, John, 10
Cape May, 21

Cedar Trees, 22, 79
Chapman, John, 12
"Chesapeake" (U. S. Frigate), 17
Clam: Broth, 110: Chowder, 110: Fritters, 108
Clams: Deviled, 109: Dried, 14
Clamtown, 1
Clamtown Sailcar, 2
Clark's Landing, 101
"Club House," 72
Coffee, 114
Coleman (or Colman), John, 9
"Conrad's," 39
Crabs, Deviled, 111
Crammer, James, 63

Decoys, 4, 79
Dingletown, 17
"Dummy," 96

Edge Cove, 2, 95
Egg Harbor Harrier, 115
"Engleside," 74

Faden, William (Map of 1777), 21
Fenimore, Francis, 85, 90
Fenimore, Jason, 4
Figure-Head, 83
Fire Backs, 107
Fish: Chowder, 112: Soup, 112
Forked River, 95
Forks of Little Egg Harbour, 99, 101
"Fortuna" (Bark), 40
Fox Burrow (Foxborough), 8, 99, 101

Great Swamp, 22, 61
"Great Swamp Long Beach Company," 64

"Guadelupe" (3000 Ton Ship), 35, 83

Haddock, John, W., 71
Harvey Cedars, 75
"Harvey Cedars Hotel," 75
Harvey Cedars Life Saving Station, 38
Hawk Tree, 79
High Point, 25
"High Point Inn," 73
"House of Refuge," 27
Hudson, Henry, 9

Indian Ann (Roberts), 17
Indian Mills, 16
Inman Whaling Lookout Tower, 24

Jennings, Captain Isaac, 81, 87

Keith, George, 11
"Kralijarca," (600 Ton Bark), 32

"Lashy" (Last Indian Brave), 16
Lawrence, John, 12
Lenni Lenape Tribe, 13
Life Saving Station: Barnegat, 31: Loveladies, 37
Lighthouse (Barnegat), 41
Little Egg Harbor Bay, 22
London Board of Trade, 29
Long Beach, (early visitors), 2
"Long Beach House," 66
"Long Beach Island Fishing Club," 38
"Long Beach Island Railroad Co.," 96
"Long Beach News" (Newspaper), 30
"Long Land Water," 10
Loveladies Life Saving Station, 32
Lovelady Island, 37

Manahawkin Bay, 22
"Manahawkin Long Beach Transportation Company," 89, 97
"Mansion of Health," 61, 62

Meade, Gen. George Gordon, 44
"Miss Bob White," 88

"New York" (Immigrant Ship), 28
Nicolls, Colonel Richard, 11
"Nova Caesarea," 11

"Ocean Emblem" (Toms River Newspaper), 29
"Oceanic Hotel," 69
"Olive," (Houseboat), 85
Oysters: Escalloped, 111: Fried, 110

"Parry House," 73
"Peahala Club," 91
"Pennsylvania Railroad," 96
"Penrose Club," 89
Perrine, Captain Samuel Forman, Sr., 27, 75, 77
Perrine, Captain Samuel Forman, Jr., 31, 75
Perrine, J. H. (Maker of Sneak Boxes), 78
"Philadelphia Company House," 61, 66
Pirate of New Jersey Coast, 25
Port of Entry, 5
Post Offices, 5, 73

Reservation (Indian), 14
Rogers, Riley, 84

Sailcar, 2, 97
Salt Pans, 7
Salt Works, 7
Sandy Hook, 9, 41
"Sans Souci" (Schooner Yacht), 31, 34, 76
School, 90
Sea Haven Light, 22
"Seven Cedars Club," 89
Shell Piles, 13
Ships' Name Boards, 82
Skeletons of Tall Indians, 18
Sneak Boxes (Floral), 86
Spencer, W. (Light Opera Composer), 88

"Stafford Beach," 74
Stations (Railroad), 90, 97
Steamboats, 2
Stew: Irish, 114: Venison, 115

"Tar Pot," 96
"Tasso," (British Bark), 27
"The Social," 70
Toms River, 95
Tucker Ebenezer, 1, 5
Tucker, Reuben, 61
Tuckerton, 1, 5

"Union Inn" (Tuckerton), 6

Verranzo, Giovanni, 10

Volunteer Life Saving Crews, 27

Watson, Thomas F., 24, 61
"West Jerseyman," (Newspaper), 28, 44
Whales, 23
Whaling, 23
White, David M., 81
Willow Landing, 6
Wind Mills, 91
Wireless Tower (Tuckerton), 3
Worley, Richard (Pirate), 25
Wreck Reports, 32

"Yellow Jacket," 96